MY MEXICAN HOME

MY MEXICAN HOME

by Graham Wilson
Copyright ©Graham Wilson
Edited by Amelia Gilliland
Printed in the United States of America
ISBN 978-1-927691-13-7

Library and Archives Canada Cataloguing in Publication
Wilson, Graham, 1962-
    My mexican home / Graham Wilson.

GRACIAS A...

Many wonderful people welcomed me to Baja. I am thankful to
the workers who built my house and the locals who helped me
feel at home. Numerous friends joined me on the adventures
described in this book. I am particularly grateful to Heather
Horsfall, Don McKnight, Stephen Kelemen, Alessandro De
Robertis, Marina Matei, Donna Eshel, Marla Hedman, Terry
Townson, Cody Peterson, Kim and Rob Cross, John and
Debbie Harper, Tony Ciprani, Jamie Fillion, Dena Marean,
Suzanne Sweetman, Mary Napier, Kim and Claudia Peterson,
Michael Thirkill, Margo and Tony Huizing, John Warren, Katie
and Scott Clapp, Richard Voss, Piera Mariani, and Deb Bergman.
My amazing daughters, Emily and Jessica Wilson, always
encourage my writing and tolerate my bad jokes.

Box 31599, Whitehorse, Yukon, Canada, Y1A 6L2

*Our relationship with Mexico is in many ways
a lot closer, and a lot more intimate and romantic,
than we have even with Canada.*
—ANTHONY BOURDAIN

A Year in Provence

When my first daughter, Emily, was born, I was 33. I had been with my wife, Lauren, for five years. While I don't believe there is a "perfect" time to start a family, it seemed as good as any. I had been active in my twenties and had climbed and whitewater kayaked all over the place. Our careers were on track, and we had a comfortable home outside of town.

I arrived early in my rusty Toyota Tercel hatchback. I needed to take home the two dozen teddy bears, flowers, and balloons friends and family had sent. After a couple of days in the hospital, they were being discharged. Lesson one, please don't give teddy bears to newborns. They're a hassle, and it takes a year before the baby even attaches to them. And when they do, the baby will attach to one or two. Give a lasagna instead—practicality triumphs sentimentality at times like these.

On my way back to the hospital, I picked up a latte for Lauren and got the car nice and warm. We strapped Emily into a rear-facing baby seat and covered her head with a blanket. March in Canada is chilly, and in northern Canada downright cold. For the first time, the sensation of having a family sank in. The responsibilities made me sweat. Lauren smiled, and I felt a sense of fulfillment I had never known.

At home, Lauren breastfed Emily on the couch while I made lunch. Both of them were voracious from the short drive. I turned on soft music as a few close friends and Lauren's twin sister took turns visiting. Emily fed whenever she was awake, and I rarely saw more than the back of her head. I busied myself making Lauren tea and snacks and helping our Lab, Milo, adjust to the change in routine. By evening we were so exhausted we couldn't see straight. When we climbed into bed, the next couple of decades seemed decided. I was a dad, and things were changing.

The peace shattered a couple of hours later. Emily screeched a mind-numbing staccato. I jumped out of bed and attempted my first-night change. Lauren handed me Emily, and I could feel her damp warmth. I had practiced on a doll in the birthing class, but it's much more difficult changing an angry, real baby. I laid her on the top of our dresser, our makeshift change table. A light blue flannelette cover over a padded vinyl mat on a simple pine IKEA dresser. Emily gasped between shrieks. Her little arms and legs were flailing. I undid the tiny snaps on her onesies. I pushed them over her arms and off her. I felt Lauren's presence over my shoulder.

"She's wet," Lauren said.

I undid the Velcro of the diaper and felt the heft of urine. I lifted her legs with my left hand and clumsily pulled the wet diaper away from her. The diaper pail, which was several feet away, was out of my reach. I stood holding the diaper in one hand and Emily's legs in the other without a plan. Lauren ended my fumbling by sliding in front of me and relieving me of my duty. She wiped Emily's bottom while I threw the diaper away. She slathered on diaper cream, and in a few swift motions, Emily was in a new diaper. Lauren snapped up her new sleepers and then swaddled her like a burrito. It looked so easy. Emily stopped crying immediately. Lauren's skill shocked us both. "There isn't any way I will ever learn to do this," I thought as I went to the kitchen to get Lauren a glass of ice water. When I returned, she was propped against the headboard with Emily sucking voraciously.

I can't think of a more useless feeling than watching your baby nurse at night. The delivery a few days earlier had been dramatic and emotional. I struggled with the dimensions of the experience. I knew deep down I could never endure the pain and sacrifice. After a couple of days in the hospital, it was now up to us. I struggled to be a help, but I was way out of my depth. As I climbed back into bed, I looked at the stack of books on my bedside.

"While Emily feeds, would you like me to read to you?" I asked Lauren.

"What do you have?" she asked.

"I have some Cormac McCarthy, but people always get murdered in those books."

"I don't want anything violent," she said. "What else do you have?"

I studied the stack and felt terrible for not having chosen something beforehand.

"There's a travel book called "A Year in Provence," I said.

"What's it about?"

"An English guy fixes up a French country house," I said.

"That," she said, fearing I would suggest a thriller, or worse, a western.

I slid back the book from near the bottom of the stack and sat beside her against the headboard.

I had never read anything by Peter Mayle. The book was a Christmas present a few months earlier. Back then, we all got hardcovers every Christmas. It was a tradition that often meant you would be reading books you might never have chosen yourself. Hardcovers were always discounted during the holidays. Most stores had stacks of them at the entrance. I received several hardcovers by writers like Grisham, Patterson, and King every season.

I had been curious about Peter Mayle's massive bestseller. It was a good choice when you brought your first child home from the hospital. Reading to my exhausted wife was the most caring thing I could think of doing. I wanted to say we will one day find a balance. But the next several months were going to be rough. We would be sleep deprived and harried the way new parents often are. But Lauren knew all this, and it was me that needed to adjust.

"A Year in Provence" is the story of a middle-aged English guy who buys a run-down farmhouse in southern France. The book is a romp through the challenges of doing a home repair in a foreign country. Mayle describes runny French cheeses and sophisticated wines. They dine on coq au vin and baguette and eat hearty stews in the nearby villages. He struggles with local tradespeople, the changing seasons, and many other obstacles. But in the year manages to complete the house.

"A Year in Provence" was hopeful. In the five years Lauren and I had been together, we had traveled lots and managed to build a house of our own. Mayle said we would be able to travel again. It also piqued my interest in renovating a home abroad. We dreamt about different places we could visit and maybe even live.

I learned to clean and change Emily better, though I never got the hang of swaddling. Emily's enormous appetite gave at least a couple of hours of reading time in the middle of each night. By the end of the week, we managed to complete "A Year in Provence." After that first week of excitement, the idea of reading during feedings lost its charm. I still did changes, but we all went back to sleep instead. Emily nursed in our bed, and we learned to sleep through it.

Dirtbag Riviera

Twenty-two years later, I'm divorced and camping on a beach in Baja. Emily and her sister, Jessica, are at university or traveling. I'm avoiding the harsh realities of the Canadian winter. I learned to kiteboard the previous season and live out of a Toyota Sienna minivan on the beach. I camperized the minivan with Emily by removing the back row of seats. We built a plywood folding bed with a cooler and storage underneath. I'm sometimes teased by friends who ask if I'm dropping the kids off at soccer. But in all honesty, the minivan suits my lifestyle well.

I usually camp on a beach a couple of miles outside the town of La Ventana. The town is popular with kiteboarders, windsurfers, and mountain bikers. Hot Springs Beach is somewhat private, with rarely more than a few campers. It's a broad sandy beach that faces an island called Isla Cerralvo. At certain tides, you can pile rocks in the sea, and hot water from a fissure in the earth fills the pool. There are five sunshades called "palapas" made from local palm leaves. In the mid-day heat, you can escape to the shade under them.

After a few months of camping on the beach, I'm restless. I don't like depending on restaurant bathrooms and rarely have access to a shower. I find the few hours immediately after dark the most difficult. I either watch movies on my phone or read on my Kindle. To sit upright, I must be in the front passenger seat. By the end of the winter, I'm feeling rough. My face is chapped and sunburnt, and my hair is a tangled, bleached mess. I live in faded board shorts and sandals. I feel homeless, which in a way, I am. I begin to dream about having a fridge and a bathroom of my own. Renting an apartment is possible. So is buying an RV or even getting a small house. I've found my paradise, but I need to figure some things out.

La Ventana is the "Heart of the Dirtbag Riviera." A Dirtbag being an adventurous person who places adrenaline sports ahead of all else. Some Dirtbags mountain bike or whitewater kayak or rock climb. La Ventana attracts a motley assortment of wind sport Dirtbags. They come from around the world. The type of person attracted to its gusty beaches are hardcore thrill seekers. They don't crave fine dining or expanded shopping opportunities. They're the type of people who wear ripped board shorts, faded T-shirts, flip flops, and trucker hats. They spend the winter in campers and vans and line-up for communal showers. Many have never spent more than thirty dollars on a haircut.

They can be twenty or seventy; their commonality is their Dirtbag sensibility. They aren't materialists except when it comes to their gear. They have quivers of expensive kites of different sizes for all wind conditions. Their mountain bikes often cost more than their cars. Educated and skilled, if they chose conventional work life, they would be wealthy. But they work seasonally or online. They try to get as many days on the water each year as possible. They have chosen this life and they don't have regrets. They are some of the happiest people I have ever met. This, for lack of a better word, is my "tribe."

La Ventana's proximity to Cabo is perfect. It's a two-hour drive—far enough to keep the tour buses away. Cabo has an international airport and most Dirtbags never venture beyond its airport.

La Ventana is also only forty-five minutes from the lovely town of La Paz. Tourists don't go to La Paz in huge numbers. It's 300,000 citizens keep the town very Mexican. La Paz has pretty much anything that you would ever need. It has great restaurants, nightclubs, and specialty stores, as well as Home Depot and Walmart. But for many in La Ventana, they only go to La Paz once a month. Dirtbags have minimal material needs.

The road cuts through the mountains and drops to the desert floor. As you turn towards town, the road bisects a sprawling forest of Cardon cacti. These distinctive plants often grow in a cluster of tall branches. The first time I drove this road, I stopped several times to marvel at the dreaminess of the landscape. The rolling hills lead to glimpses of the sea and myriad bright kites dancing in the breeze. For a confused guy from the north, this setting was as close to divine as I had known.

As you approach town, there are several colourful cinderblock buildings offering kite repairs, lessons, and rooms. Restaurants, grocery stores, and Mexican handicraft stores are also here and there. But the real essence of this town is a campground in the middle of the beach. This campground has been a fixture for years. The coveted "Front Row" or the campsites bordering the beach, often staked out by October. Expensive RVs park cheek to jowl. Between them, beige "Costco tents" for drying kites suck up all the available space. Three large rectangular bathroom buildings are along the fence at the back. Sprinter vans and off-grid motorhomes are the most common vehicles. But there is a smattering of Volkswagen vans and old trailers. A handful of people have tents, but the vast majority live comfortably in expensive RVs. Most have been spending winters here for years.

The hardware stores in La Ventana are always busy. The locals buy bags of cement, cinderblock, and pipe. The gringos search for stainless steel screws for their kiteboards or parts for their unreliable refrigerators. The walls of the hardware store are covered with tools and supplies and often require ladders to reach. There are several grocery stores with the most popular being Star Market and Oscaritos. They belong to the same family and stock similar inventory. Oscaritos is much larger while Star Market is more conveniently located. The OXXO carries cold beer and junk food and is where you can buy cellphone minutes. Oddly, there's only one fish store in town. When the seas are rough, its coolers are empty because the fisherman are unable to launch or work their nets.

The new restaurants offer vegan fare and have names like Namaste or Nomada. It's now easy to get a quality espresso or an eight-dollar artisanal loaf of bread. Green grocers hawk produce with prices to match southern California. You can rent high-end mountain bikes and take workshops on artisanal cheese making, organic gardening, or small-market wine making. You rarely see locals partake in these offerings.

The other end of the strip is El Sargento. La Ventana was one ranch and El Sargento another. Now they have merged. El Sargento is where the locals live. You'll notice the food kiosks and restaurants sell more traditional fare. Carts offering tripe tacos, pizza, and hot dogs always seem to have customers.

The locals tend to live in simple cinderblock homes in El Sargento. There is a church, a school, baseball and soccer fields. The gringos live in an array of buildings all vying for ocean views. Some of these homes cost hundreds of thousands of dollars and resemble what you find in upscale communities in southern California. This is especially true close to the beach with several million-dollar homes built in recent years.

Every morning I go to a shop called Kijote Coffee. I visit friends and check email while drinking my Grande Americano con Leche. Beside the coffee shop is a real estate agency. In their front window are listings of local houses for sale. The listings are generally for big homes that don't interest me. I'm window shopping and only vaguely interested. I don't want anything expensive, and since I'm alone, I don't need much space. Many of us didn't want to make our winter escape look anything like the houses we've left in the north. I want something simpler and more "Mexican."

While sipping my coffee, I think about Peter Mayle and "A Year in Provence." That simple story has festered in my subconscious for decades. Finding a modest house and renovating in the local style interests me. I think about having an outdoor kitchen and growing my own vegetables. Like Peter Mayle, I will hire day laborers and have a cross-cultural romp. It's tantalizing, but I wonder if I'm being realistic. As a result, I keep this dream to myself.

There are small local homes available in town. Owned by Mexican families and sold privately, often through word of mouth. They're usually found in the community of El Sargento, which borders La Ventana. These houses are simple and usually didn't have views. The locals are practical and live within walking distance of the school or church. They're part of a tight-knit community. I've met a few gringos who had bought houses in El Sargento. Barking dogs, roosters, and the dreaded all-night quinceañeras eventually pushed them to get houses closer to the beach. It seems like an unsolvable problem, and I start to consider RVs and even look at a few. But a thirty-foot Winnebago isn't for me either.

The realtor beside the coffee shop also has columns of listings for undeveloped land.

The lots look identical to each other: scrub desert with views of the turquoise sea. Buying a vacant lot requires working with an architect and construction company. It's a complicated endeavour and doesn't interest me much.

Undeterred, I hunt for an abandoned or neglected home I can renovate. I want a traditional Mexican house that's private and has a view. This is a tall order. Few locals choose the inconvenience of living away from their family and friends.

One day, I hear about an unfinished house a school teacher from La Paz built. It's empty and a short distance from the central part of town. It has a commanding view of the Sea of Cortez too. It sounds too good to be true. The person who told me about it has never been there and only has a vague idea of where it is. I debate the story's veracity for about a week until one afternoon, feeling bored, I go in search of it. I crisscross the dusty desert roads on the west side of town. Dirt paths weave between cactus and Palo Blanco trees in a haphazard grid. My van scrapes against branches and gets "Baja pin-striping." For the better part of an afternoon, I explore every dirt road I can find. Then I spot a lone house in the middle of a broad hill.

It pokes out of the desert's low canopy, revealing a boxy-looking two-story house. It's grey with unpainted stucco. A ten-foot carved wooden sign at the front of the yard is strung between a couple of tall posts. It reads "Vista Marina" or ocean view. I know I'm in the right place.

I park in front of a barbed-wire rancher's fence. I untwist a rusty clasp that holds the gate somehow without cutting my hands. The yard is overgrown with an array of bushes, trees, and cacti. Along the side stands a row of nine coconut palms about twelve feet tall. The yard once had intent but is now long forgotten, overgrown, and unkept.

The house is strange looking. A small second-floor hovers over a breezeway downstairs. There appears to be parking in the breezeway. Shaded parking would be nice in this desert. But it has ornate floor tiles that would shatter under the weight of a vehicle.

There is a bathroom and a shower room downstairs behind locked, barred doors. The other wall is support for the upstairs. Like many traditional Mexican homes, there are stairs on the outside. They wrap around the building and climb to a landing. Long sliding glass doors with a locked exterior door stop me from going farther. The sliding doors on both sides of the room have bullet holes and make the building seem neglected.

I can see much of the room from the landing. The Sea of Cortez glistens through the sliding doors on the other side of the room. A bed along this wall will have an unobstructed sunrise and sunset view. There appears to be a small bathroom on the right side of the room, though I can't see into it. It's an airy bedroom with windows on all sides, and it'll be breezy on warm summer nights.

I walk back downstairs to the front of the building. If the downstairs was enclosed, it would be fantastic, I think. An addition would give a good kitchen/dining room/living room. Additionally, it would have a deck area off the bedroom with an expansive view of the bay. Immediately, I see the potential of the building and know it's a rarity in La Ventana. Finishing the house will be easy, I think.

I walk into the backyard and noticed a steel ladder leading to the roof, bolted to the side of the building. I pull on it to make sure it will support my weight. It doesn't budge, so I climb its rungs. The rooftop reveals the best view in the Baja. The desert spreads to the Sea of Cortez with Isla Cerralvo in the distance. I can see a distant lighthouse and the mountains that surround the valley. It's breathtaking, and after half an hour, I climb back down, thrilled with my find. Since there isn't much else to see, I sit in the shade of a magnificent Palo Blanco tree beside the house. I know this house has to be mine.

I phone Chava, a local builder I met a year earlier. He tells me that the house is for sale and has been empty since it was built seven years before. Chava has seen it once, but that was years ago. He says he will make some calls, and we make plans to meet at the house the next day. I go to bed like a kid on Christmas Eve. I don't know the price or any other details, but I have a good feeling about the house. I fall asleep listening to the surf and dreaming of finishing the place.

When I return in the morning, Chava is already at the house. He's on the roof, and I climb the ladder to join him. On the top, the view seems even more magnificent. Sunlight sheets off the sea in a blinding glare, and a cool breeze makes my skin tingle.

"It's beautiful," says Chava with a broad smile. "Chingon!" is how the locals say "amazing."

He tells me he hasn't reached the owner. But he heard the price of the house is $25,000.

"Chingon," I say.

I have a line of credit and can transfer that amount to my checking account. I tell Chava to make the necessary arrangements with the seller, and we fist bump. I'm ecstatic as Chava and I climb to the yard. We discuss adding the addition and some of the other required improvements. It all seems very doable. Chava says that he isn't busy, and all the work can be finished quickly. I ask him to give me a price to make it liveable.

The house is on untitled property. After agrarian reform, the Mexican government formed communal bodies called "Ejido's." The Ejido in El Sargento governs this property. Ten years earlier, they allowed gringos to buy land. These tracts were being divided into lots for vacation homes. To get title, you had to form a trust called a fideicomiso and apply to the central government in Mexico City. This process costs a few thousand dollars and often takes a few years. In the end, you have title and will have to pay five hundred dollars in annual property taxes. I'm all right with a long-term lease and, at some point, applying for title. Ejido land is inexpensive because the process is more complicated. For me, it all seems part of the adventure.

Chava asks if I want to see his farm. It's outside the village of Los Planes, five miles south of La Ventana. We get into the van, and we drive through the Cardon forest. Los Planes supplies vegetables to La Paz and other communities in Baja. It's surrounded by mountains. The rich alluvial soil is irrigated by arroyos replenished in the rainy season. This is a fertile valley.

We drive down a wide dirt road a short distance from his father's house and park. His land is a triangular-shaped piece of dirt next to his father's vast fields of green. Chava's father grows alfalfa. He harvests every month, and many sprinklers spray his fields. Chava's tiny patch in comparison is undeveloped, arid, and brown.

"My father has free water from the arroyo," says Chava.

"Where will you get water?" I ask.

"I'm lucky the arroyo comes close. I will collect water in the rainy season."

Chava leads me to a trench he's dug. It's the size of an Olympic pool, and I'm surprised he dug this by hand.

"When the arroyo floods, I will pump water into here," he says, pointing at the pit.

"But won't the water leak out?" I ask.

"I will line it with a membrane," he says. "Then I will have free water most of the dry season"

Chava shows me a table with seedlings growing in red plastic solo cups. He's experimenting with what plants are suited to his land. It's all very low tech, and he's enthusiastic about developing a farm of his own. "Would you like to see a big Cardon?" He asks.

We get in the van and, after a kilometre, reach a kink in the road. On the side, a massive Cardon looms. I have never seen one as big as this. We get out of the van and marvel at the dozens of arms and the thickness of its base.

"It's at least seven hundred years old," Chava says.

"That means it was growing before Cortez even came to Mexico," I say.

"Si, it's ancient."

We walk around it for a few minutes, and I take photos of Chava standing in front of it for scale.

"I have seen much bigger," he says.

We get back in the van, and I turn it around on the narrow dirt track. Once on the highway, Chava points to a nondescript cinderblock building. It has high walls and iron grating. Several rooms radiate off a central courtyard.

"That's a whore house," he says.

I had driven past the building many times and never knew what it was.

"I would have never guessed that," I say.

"Si," he says.

"What would it be like if I went there," I ask.

"If they like you, they will give you tequila and get you drunk. Then a prostitute will take you into a room for the night. And you'd give them $100."

That sounds about right, I think.

"But if they really like you," he continues, "they will get you drunk, hit you over the head, and take all your money."

"No, no, I want the first one," I say, laughing.

Chava is full of those sorts of stories. He told me about his years as a mariachi traveling around Baja, sometimes even playing in the lavish palaces of narcos. His stories fill the gaps in my understanding of Baja.

I visit the house every day and think about improving it. Later in the week, a taciturn older man, a representative of the Ejido, and a notary meet me at the house. We shake hands. They don't speak a word of English, so Chava translates. Documents are signed and notarized. After I hand over an envelope with a few thousand dollars, the house is mine. It's quick and painless.

Chava and I drive to La Paz to have the documents filed. I need to have my passport and tourist card photocopied and others notarized. I have heard horror stories about Mexican bureaucracy. And I know I'm taking a risk not having a lawyer handle the transfer. But I feel comfortable with the process. While losing my investment is a possibility, I've bought a house for less than the price of a new car.

I start transferring the remaining twenty-two thousand dollars from my chequing account to the seller's bank. This is more complicated than anticipated. Mexico monitors large transactions, looking for narco money and untaxed revenues. But after several trips to the bank and some lengthy phone calls with my bank back home, the house is mine.

I drive to Star Market to pick up some cold beer to celebrate with a couple of friends. While standing in line to pay, I see Tony. He's a fixture in this community and has been coming here for decades. He's owned a few houses and has worked with Chava.

"Did you hear? I bought a house," I say.

"Where?" he asks.

"It's in Centro, about a kilometre away from OXXO," I say.

"Sounds great," he says.

"It needs work, but it will be great," I say.

"Who's doing the work?" he asks.

"Chava is doing the first things," I say.

"The problem is all the best tradesmen work for the big construction companies," he says. "The ones that remain are the B-squad."

"I've heard that," I say.

"It can be a real struggle working with some of them," he says, stepping to the till and paying for his few items. After he pays, he wishes me the best and leaves. I pay for the beer and return to the house.

At that moment, I have a terrible case of buyer's remorse. Like a curtain being yanked, my mood sinks.

"What have I got myself into?" I wonder.

I curse Peter Mayle and his stuffy life in the French countryside. His ridiculous romp from one charcuterie board to the next. Baja isn't Provence, and I fear the uncertainty of navigating these waters. The simplicity of living in my old Sienna minivan on the beach suddenly seems irresistibly attractive.

Moving In

The morning sun is blasting the front of the house when I arrive. I park outside the gate and examine the rancher's fence that surrounds the yard. Four strands of barbed wire are strung on posts five feet high. Every couple of feet are vertical branches and rusty poles to deter cows. In one corner, a display for batteries wired to the fence. "Energizer" written across the top. On either side of the gate are fifteen-foot wood posts ten inches in diameter. Strung between them is a twelve-foot sign about a foot wide. It reads "Vista Marina." It's a cliche and I can't wait to replace it. Names matter.

I open the gate and walk to the house. I go upstairs and open the sliding doors and windows. I fumble with the keys to the downstairs bathrooms. The rooms are stuffy with lots of cobwebs and dust. I get a broom and dustpan from the van and start sweeping. I carry a jug in from the van and add cleanser to a bucket of water. I start mopping—the pine scent masking the muskiness of the building.

I take a foam mattress and bedding from the van and make a bed. It's the first night in my home. I feel fortunate to have found it.

When the sun finally sets, I make myself a sandwich while wearing a headlamp. I wash it down with an icy Pacifico beer. The perfect first day, as I climb into bed and read Don Quixote on my Kindle. Twenty minutes later, I'm fast asleep, and it isn't even eight o'clock.

Shortly after midnight, I wake to a sharp sting on my left shoulder. Instinctively, I slap at the bite. A squirming insect about an inch long is under my fingers. I jump out of bed and fumble for the flashlight. On my throbbing shoulder is a small dot of blood in a welt. In my bed, an injured scorpion writhes. I grab my sandal and push the scorpion onto the floor. I smash it until it's a pulpy mess. I'm breathing hard. The bite has an intensity far worse than any bee sting I have ever had. I have never had a scorpion bite and know that sometimes they can be fatal. I pick up my phone and Google: "scorpion sting," "scorpion sting fatal," "scorpion sting hospital." I learn that I'm all right but might be sore for a few days. I search the bedroom for others. High on the wall near my bed is another. It is about fifty percent larger than the one that stung me. I throw my sandal at it, making a direct hit. The scorpion hits the floor and, with its two front pincers raised and its tail curled, is ready to attack. I grab my sandal and slam it a few times until I'm sure it's dead. I walk around the room and, at the back wall, find a third the size of the first one—I pulp it with my sandal. The rest of the night is a twilight sleep.

I read that while scorpions are solitary animals, they sometimes travel in gangs of thirty. The larger ones could be fifteen years or older. The young ride on their mother's backs until their first molt, and then they're on their own. Scorpions are cousins to spiders and have eight legs and hunt at night. They were likely at my house in search of water. In my research, I learned that scorpions luminesce under black light. For this reason, they are easy to catch at night if you have a suitable flashlight.

At daybreak, I drive to Ace Hardware in downtown La Paz. I always find this hardware has the odds and ends that are difficult to find elsewhere. Since they won't be open for a couple of hours, I go to Restaurant La Catholica. This mainstay breakfast joint is popular because of their chilaquiles. This meal is either a tomato or tomatillo sauce poured over tortillas. I always order the red chilaquiles with eggs. This simple meal can be transcendent, and La Catholica prepares it better than anyone. I order a vampire to start. This drink is half orange juice and half beet juice and is sweet and unctuous. Soon, I had a delicious plate of chilaquiles in front of me. It makes my lack of sleep less jarring, and I feel much better with each mouthful.

When Ace Hardware opens, I'm the first customer in the store. The clerk who unlocked the door greets me and asks if I need anything. I tell him I need a "scorpion light," which is the best I could do with my limited Spanish. I'm sure he's tired of gringos with scorpion bites waiting outside his door every morning when he opens. He leads me to the front counter, where there is an entire display of scorpion flashlights next to the till. The small purple LED flashlight has an engraved icon of a scorpion on its shaft. The clerk turns it on, but in the daylight, it doesn't look impressive. I hand him some cash and leave the store confident I'm taking a step in the right direction.

When it's dark enough, I check my entire house. I go through my bedroom first but don't find any. On the upstairs deck, I find one scorpion climbing the wall. I go downstairs and get a shovel to reach it, and with a slight pinging sound, it's dead. I then go to the kitchen and find two more. Once again, I take off my sandal and pound them. I walk outside and shine the light on the back perimeter of the house. A small scorpion glows, and I get my shovel and beat it to death. Several feet away, I find another one that is four inches long and was the largest I've seen yet. I walk around my yard and find almost two dozen more. Some are on the ground and motionless. Others walk on the sticks of the fence. I see scorpions climbing the walls of my house and even trying to walk up the stairs to my bedroom. For the next half hour, I crush as many as I can find. I pound them until I'm sure they're dead. It's a gruesome situation. I have a severe infestation.

Drinking my coffee the following day, I dread nightfall. Hitting them with a shovel killed them, but it required me to place the flashlight in my mouth to use both hands. Sometimes it was difficult to reach the shovel if the scorpions were in cactus or the bark of a branch. I go to the hardware store and buy a tall can of the equivalent of Raid.

That night, I find another twenty scorpions in my yard but only one in my house. It feels like progress but only slightly. The Raid kills the small ones immediately, but the large scorpions writhe for five minutes or more. It seems cruel, but I'm desperate.

The sign over my entrance gate read "Vista Marina." It was cliche, I thought. Often, the names of houses in Mexico seem cheesy and predictable. They usually describe a view or a cactus. Names matter. It's an endearment; an intention. I was a fan of "*The Simpsons*" for years. Marge has a nervous breakdown in one episode and recovers at a spa called

Rancho Relaxo. The final scene was Marge in a bubble bath, eating an ice cream sundae and drinking a bottle of tequila. This scene encompasses everything I believe to be true and holy. A silly and irreverent homage.

So, I take out my laptop and design a sign for "Rancho Relaxo." I try many typefaces before settling on a decorative display font called "Fajita." I add stars on both sides of the lettering for ornamentation. It's over-the-top and fun.

I had heard that there was a new furniture maker in town. He has a little storefront with a few pieces in it, but he mostly does custom work. He's supposed to be a nice guy and speaks good English. So, I go over to his shop, which is on the main drag. He's busy restoring an old dresser. When I arrive, he's sanding by hand. It's ornate and has a lot of scrollwork. As I enter the yard, a thin, friendly man approaches.

"Do you make signs?" I ask.

"What would you like?"

I tell him that I live nearby and need a large wooden sign to replace the one I have. Lucas suggests seeing the old sign in person. He locks up his shop, and we get in the van and drive up the hill. We park outside the gate, and Lucas looks at the view.

"Very beautiful," he says.

"But I don't like the name Vista Marina," I explain.

He agrees and asks what I want to call the house.

"Rancho Relaxo," I say.

Lucas looks confused.

"It's from *The Simpson's,*" I say, passing him my phone with a YouTube clip of Marge in the tub. He watches the clip and laughs. I show him the graphic on the laptop, and he likes the font and the stars.

"I want this sign to replace that sign," I say, pointing at the Vista Marina sign.

Lucas says the wood and the carving will cost $70 and about a week to complete. I hand him a deposit and drive him back to his shop.

I go on another scorpion-killing spree that night. Maybe they're traveling in gangs? I go to sleep with my scorpion flashlight beside my pillow. I wake in the middle of the night to a rhythmic crunching sound. I turn on the flashlight and look around the room without getting out of bed. Two eyes glow from the deck.

"Is that a cat?" I wonder.

I soon realize it's a fox. It has rich auburn hair, a thin face, and a hare dangling from its mouth. Not wanting to scare the fox, I turn off the flashlight. I watch it tear apart the hare in the moonlight through the glass door. It feels strange to have a fox six feet away, but I've seen lots of foxes back home. It gnaws on the hare, and I fall back asleep. When I wake, I wonder if I dreamt the entire thing. But when I open the door to the deck, one of the hare's forearms lays on the threshold of the door. The fox was sharing a morsel of meat with me. I pick up the leg and chuck it into the desert. The wilderness must have been reclaiming the house for years, I think.

Chava stops by later in the morning to discuss how to finish the house. He has some excellent ideas, and we agree on most things. Chava explains what "universal size" means in Mexico. It's a ratio of room sizes that are common. Most traditional Mexican homes have similar-sized rooms. I have an oversized open breezeway, which I want to convert into a kitchen with an island. The size of the living room will be the existing width of the kitchen. I don't know a lot about architecture, but I understand that room proportions matter. Tacking an enormous living room onto a tiny house would be odd. This situation is exacerbated because the upstairs deck will be the exact same dimensions. Chava explains that gringos often want decks much larger than Mexicans. I agree with him, as my decks back home are almost half the square footage of my house.

Chava walks into the desert and stops.

"This is where a Mexican would put the wall," he says, scuffing the dirt with his foot.

"That looks okay," I say.

"You come here, and I will go there," he says. We exchange positions, and I stand on his scuff mark.

"Take one step back," he tells me. And I step backwards.

"Come back a little," he says. We go back and forth like this a few more times and finally decide where to put the wall. I make a final scuff mark and then pick up a couple of softball-sized rocks to mark its location. We have designed the addition without a tape measure, pad, or pencil.

"I would like a big window so you can see the sea while you eat," I explain.

"Not too big because that's a southern exposure, and the room will get too hot," he cautions.

"Not too big but opening so you can feel the breeze," I say.

"Chingon," he says.

We study the size of the addition and review the other things as well. I want the kitchen to be L-shaped with an island. The island will be wide enough for a couple of stools to be a nook. The kitchen floor needs to be removed, and a new one for the entire downstairs poured. I need a storage area beside the house called a bodega to store my bike and kites.

"How much will all this cost," I ask.

"Well, it's a lot of things," Chava says. After a long pause, "$12,000."

This estimate is lower than I expected.

"How long will it take?" I ask.

"Four, five weeks," he says.

"That would be great because I leave in May for the summer," I say.

"Everything done before you leave," he promises.

"Okay, so a month and $12,000," I confirm.

"Si," he says.

"I'll go to La Paz and start getting you money. The ATM only lets me take out a thousand dollars a day."

"Then I can start by the end of the week," he says, shaking my hand.

"$12,000 and five weeks to complete this list," I say, passing my list to him.

"Chingon," he says.

After he leaves, I drive to La Paz and withdraw cash from the bank. I'm going down the Malecon in a line of slow traffic. I notice a traffic cop who has extorted bribes from me and some of my friends in the past. He's standing on the other side of the intersection. I stop and then creep through the intersection

"Shit," I say to myself as he waves me over. I reach into my glove box and get my insurance and registration and take my driver's license out of my wallet.

He strolls to my open window

"Is there a problem?" I ask.

"You didn't come to a complete stop," he says, taking my documents.

"No, I did come to a complete stop," I reply.

He goes back to his car and appears to speak into his radio. It's hot, and since the van's air-conditioning doesn't work, I turn off the engine. I cover my legs from the intense sun with a T-shirt that was on the back seat. When he comes back to the van, he says I'm in big trouble because I failed to come to a complete stop. "You could have hurt some-body," he chastises. He explains the ticket is going to be very expensive.

"You will have to go to the police station and see the judge," he says. "But you can pay your ticket here if you want. It's a thousand pesos."

That's fifty dollars, I think.

"Please give me a ticket," I say.

"Then you will have to go to the police station," he says.

"Fine, let's go to the police station."

He walks back to his car and sits in the front seat, reading something.

I sit in the sweltering heat for another ten minutes before he returns.

"You pay me a thousand pesos, and you can go."

"Please give me a ticket," I say.

"You must pay the ticket here," he says.

"I'm not giving you a bribe; please give me a ticket," I reply.

Again, he walks back to his car for a couple of minutes. I'm starting to overheat and get frustrated.

"You are in big trouble and must give me the money," he says, raising his voice as he walks towards me. "You could kill somebody by not stopping at a stop sign."

"Just give me a fucking ticket!" I say in exasperation.

The cop's tone changes, and he leans in.

"Gringos that talk like you disappear," he says menacingly.

"Are you fucking threatening me?" I scream. "Is that what you're doing? Are you fucking threatening my life?"

He looks startled and doesn't say anything. He then stretches his hand towards me. I shake his hand, and he passes me my papers and says I can go. I start the van and pull away from the intersection, vowing to avoid the Malecon from now on. Two months later, the police chief and two other cops are gunned down less than a block from where I was stopped. To clean up rampant corruption, a hundred police are fired in southern Baja shortly afterwards. I never saw that cop again.

The next afternoon, Chava phones. "I've got bad news. Your house is going to cost much more to build," he says.

"How much more?" I ask

"It's going to cost $25,000."

"That's more than double what you said."

"Well, I forgot some things, and everything is more expensive now," he struggles to explain. Suspicious that he's just doubled his estimate, I take a breath.

"That's much more than I expected," I say.

"There's no way I could build for a peso less," Chava says.

"Clearly, I don't understand what things cost here," I say.

"It always costs more than you think," he explains.

"I need to get other estimates and learn more," I explain. "I'll build next season."

"I understand," he says. "Sorry, Compa,"

"Thanks for all your help, Chava, I'll be in touch," I hang up the phone.

I put the envelope of cash into the glove box of the van and go into town for a taco. Emily is arriving in six weeks. It would be easier to spend time with her without managing construction. I consider my options as I eat my lunch and soon feel better.

"It's not meant to be," I think.

Lucas calls a few minutes later and says my sign is ready. Since I'm only a block away, I tell him I will be right over. This brightens my mood, and I drive to his shop. Propped against the wall is the sign. Lucas picks it up and holds it for me to see. Instead of painting the engraved areas, he burned them. The charcoal naturally blackened the recessed lettering. The wood stained with a simple oil finish. There are three large holes along the top for the rope. It's stunning, and I thank him.

I spend the next few days hunting scorpions and landscaping my yard. I have a large Palo Blanco tree in my backyard and love its white bark. I also have a few elephant trees and a variety of other plants that I'm unfamiliar with. Along the back fence is a row of native palms, which don't need watering or care. While slow growing, they will give privacy in ten years when I will likely have neighbours. In contrast, I have nine coconut palms that require watering and care. These things have to go, I think. I rake between the trees and prune dead leaves, content to be improving the yard.

The following morning, Chava calls to say that he can honour the original estimate.

"How can you be off by double?" I ask.

"I can do everything for $12,000, and it will take a month," he says.

"Not $25,000?" I ask.

"No, $12,000," he assures me.

He helped me with the sale, and I thought of him as a friend.

"Okay. I have a thousand dollars here. You'll need to buy materials," I say.

"You'll be happy," he says. "Your house will be chingon."

Twenty minutes later, Chava arrives

"$12,000?" I say.

"Yes, everything for $12,000."

I hand him a thousand-dollar deposit, and we're in business. I return to La Paz for another withdrawal at the ATM.

Early one morning, a load of crushed gravel, sand, and cement arrives. An old water tank is dropped off, and a water truck climbs the hill and fills it. Chava stands behind a transit, and Carlos drags markers around the yard. Soon, a trench to the dimensions we had scuffed earlier in the week is dug. In the afternoon, rebar is wired together. By dinner, they are ready to pour concrete.

Chava pulls a gasoline-powered cement mixer to the house behind his car in the morning. Carlos and two other men start mixing bags of cement with water, gravel, and sand. They take turns pushing heavy wheelbarrows and shovelling cement into the footings. An hour later, the footings are done. A truck lowers a couple of palettes of cinder blocks near the footings.

After a few days, I stop going to the ATM in La Paz. I don't want to extend more money than needed. Also, I want to avoid corrupt traffic cops. The first rounds of cinder-block went up, and by the weekend, it was impressive. In the evenings, I get out my level to ensure the walls are true, and they always are. It amazes me how precise the work is considering their simple tools. I am confident that Chava was correct to follow the Universal Size. The addition looked proportional to the rest of the house.

In a week, the walls to the addition are up, and they're pouring the corners with concrete and rebar for strength. While the concrete cures, Chava and Carlos connect rebar for the ceiling. They lay these on top of the walls in a meter-wide matrix. Men show up with plywood that Chava has rented. Using two by fours, the plywood is braced from below to make the ceiling. Then thick blocks of styrofoam are placed in between the rebar. This will lighten the ceiling and reduce the amount of concrete needed.

The following day, six men from the village arrive. Carlos mans the cement mixer. Five-gallon plastic pails are filled and passed up the ladder hand to hand like old-time firemen. The men strain under the weight of the cement.

"Surely, they could find a cement truck somewhere in town?" I think.

By early afternoon, the ceiling is finished, and friends from La Paz visit. We sit in the bedroom drinking beer and looking at the deck. I can't wait for the concrete to cure so I can sit outside. The view from the deck is expansive.

I buy locally made deck furniture from a guy on the
roadside. He's from the mainland and builds a type of stick
furniture. It almost looks like wicker if you squinted your
eyes, but a lot chunkier and more durable. I look at a love
seat, couch, chair and a little table for a few hundred dollars.
When he isn't selling furniture, he's sitting beside his truck,
cutting and bending wood. I examine the furniture and offer
him a slightly lower price. But he counters with the original
price. It's a fair price, so I agree. He says he has to treat the
furniture to protect it from termites and to come back the
next day.

The following day, I drive back to his stand. My furniture is sitting beside his truck. He says that his truck broke
down and he couldn't get the supplies needed to treat the
wood. He jumps in the van, and we drive to the gas station
where he buys a half litre of diesel and a half litre of gasoline.

At his truck, he mixes the two together. He brushes the
stinky solution on the furniture. He says that the residue will
permanently repel termites. I've heard of people returning
to La Ventana to find dust where their furniture had been.
The next day, I drive the furniture to my house with the van
windows open. The fumes are horrible, and I hope it will
improve soon. I carry the furniture to the deck to air out.

I go to bed that night wondering how I'll upholster the
deck furniture. A lot of expats go with brightly coloured
patterns, hibiscus leaves, and pineapples, but that isn't what I
want. So, the next day I go to a fabric store in La Paz. I buy
a few meters of a durable exterior fabric that almost looks
like tweed. It's sand coloured like the desert. I have some old
pillows in the van that are yellow, red, and green. The upholsterers take a week to make the cushions and they're exactly

what I want. Since the furniture no longer smells of petrol, I put the cushions on the furniture and get comfortable on the deck.

Many of the older hotels and restaurants in La Paz have floors tiled with mosaicos, an ancient way to make concrete tiles. I ask around and learn that it had once been popular but was now a dying art in Baja. You can import expensive mosaicos from artisans on the mainland but getting them locally is difficult. I thought these tiles would make a nice backsplash in the kitchen.

I hear there are a couple of guys making mosaicos in the old section of town behind the Cathedral. It's a part of town I don't know well but have always found interesting.

After going to the bank, I park next to the Cathedral. I ask anyone I see if they know where I can buy mosaicos. Most have no suggestions, but a couple of people point vaguely in the same direction. I eventually find a house with a display of mosaicos. A rusty steel rack holds a couple of dozen colorful mosaicos of different sizes. They're either solid colors or a strange swirl pattern. While interesting, none of them suit my taste. I asked a man at the side of the house if knows anyone else making mosaicos. He enthusiastically tells me that there is an elderly man a couple of streets over. He points in the direction that I have to go.

I walk up and down the streets for an hour before noticing faded lettering on the front of a building. It reads "Mosaicos" in an ornate font and is faded almost to be unrecognizable. I walk into the yard and a dog on a chain barks and bares its teeth. An old man steps out of the house and yells at the dog. The dog quiets and climbs into the shade of a derelict car. This house is ramshackle, and an array of scrap metal and old cars are scattered around the yard. Everything is rusty and decrepit.

"Hi! Do you make mosaicos?" I ask.

"All my life," he replies.

He leads me to the back of the yard where there is a large mosaico press. To make them, they pour paints into a metal mold, then wet cement is added on top. A hydraulic press squishes everything together, making the tile. Unlike ceramics, the tiles don't require glazes or firing. It's a simple process once popular throughout the Old World and brought to Mexico with colonization.

I follow the man back to the house and we sit on his porch. He still has one mold and he shows it to me. It is heavy and worn. The pattern is a starburst pattern in which four tiles complete the star. He has one tile in this pattern leaning against the wall. The background is white and has two-tone blue star shapes. He passes it to me. It's exactly what I want for my backsplash, I think.

"You can have any colours," he says.

"I like these colours," I say. "I need 35 tiles."

"That will cost $35," he says.

I'm surprised by the ridiculously low price and give him the money.

"Thank you," he says. "Come back in two weeks."

"Thank you," I say, shaking his hand.

I walk back to the van elated. It's almost dinner time and I'm eager to get home and see the progress.

I'm in a video chat with a television producer in LA a few days later. She's creating episodes of the popular HGTV series *House Hunters International*. She tells me they're interested in producing an episode about an off-grid Baja beach house. Since my house will have solar electricity and solar hot water, it fits the bill. She explains that they would be showing me three houses, one of them being my house. I'd look at the places and then choose my house. All I needed was a wingman—someone to explain what they thought was best for me to the audience.

After the call ends, I watch an episode on YouTube. I have never seen *House Hunters International* before. I like the idea of promoting building small, off-grid homes. I email Emily, asking her to be my "wingman." After finishing her bachelor's degree, she took a three-month bicycle trip in Patagonia. Emily was planning to visit Baja on her way back to Canada anyway. Later that afternoon, I called her.

"I can't believe you want me to be on reality TV," she says.

"I'm not offering you crack," I reply. "It'll be fun."

"I can't believe you're even asking me," she says.

"I thought it would be a good story to tell people," I argue. "It won't take a lot of time."

But Emily's mind is made-up. She always has strong opinions.

Instead, I ask a friend who had built one of the most spectacular houses in town. She's a retired lawyer, and her house has many Colonial Mexican flourishes. She tells me that *House Hunters International* is her favourite show, and she would love to help.

I meet with Chava and tell him he has three weeks to finish his work before the film crew arrives. It's in line with our five-week schedule, I explain. Besides, it could help promote his business. Chava agrees to pick up the pace.

"It's when you said you would be finished anyways," I tell him.

"Si," he says.

"Is there a problem?" I press.

"No problem," he assures me.

But I knew there might be muchos problemas.

I email the producer and tell her my friend will be my wingman rather than Emily. I also tell her that the builders think they'll be done in time. The last part bothers me because I know I'm being optimistic.

The following week progress on the house slows. It's getting hotter, and Chava's crew thins with only him and Carlos often working alone. A couple of men from the village show up one day. Using sledgehammers and shovels, they bash the concrete on the kitchen floor. It's slow going, and I question why they don't rent a jackhammer for a couple of hours. Chava tells me this is the way they prefer to work. Their approach seems ridiculously labor-intensive and slow.

"But there are easier ways to do the same thing," I argue.

"This is better," he says.

The men beat on the cement floor for days. When they're done, the footings for the back wall of the kitchen are poured. A few days later, a cinderblock wall with a window and door frame is in place.

Being on-site is becoming difficult for me. I try to work on clearing garbage or landscaping but tire quickly. I learn the importance of not overheating in the first place. The crew seems to work slow but stays busy most of the day. I do jobs at the time of the day when they're in the shade. It's a good strategy that makes me feel better.

Chava continues to fall behind. A week later, I send an email to the producer telling her the house is progressing slowly. I suggest we film during the summer or in the fall. I never hear from her again.

Emily arrives, and we spend a couple of weeks swimming and reconnecting. She needs to recover from her trip, and a laid-back visit with her middle-aged father fits the bill. We go to jazz concerts in La Paz and all my favourite restaurants. She meets Chava and seems to like the house.

Once the kitchen floor is demoed, it's raked and smoothed. The men who poured the ceiling return, and bucket after bucket of concrete is poured. The house is looking much more complete. Chava says they're ninety percent done, but I know he is generously rounding up. He's weeks behind.

I am building my house on a 180-day tourist visa. When you enter Mexico, you get a $30 visa called an FMM. When you go through customs, you can request up to 180 days. Mexico is generous this way. Many ex-pats renew their visas twice a year, never bothering to apply for residency. It's a straightforward and inexpensive way to stay indefinitely in Mexico. But my visa is about to expire, and I need to go home to escape the heat anyways.

One afternoon, I pick up the mosaicos. Unfortunately, the old man is napping when I arrive. His grandson leads me to where the dog had been chained a couple of weeks earlier. Leaning against the fence are my mosaicos. I pick one up and the colours are vibrant and rich. It is even more beautiful than the tile he had shown me on his porch. "So beautiful," I tell the grandson. He shrugs and helps me carry them to the van. I put them on the floor of the passenger seats. I didn't want to risk damaging any on the ride home. I thank the boy and am on my way.

Carlos and Chava are starting to stucco the walls. Soon, the cement couch and cement kitchen will be built. They still need to finish the bodega, but that won't take long. The exterior doors and windows are due to be installed in the next few days. Chava is confident that within two weeks, everything will be complete. I decide to pay him the balance owed before the work is complete. I don't want to leave money with friends to pay him because that seems awkward and unnecessary. Wiring money to Mexico was challenging when I bought the house. I could only transfer a thousand dollars Canadian a day. With the exchange, this came to about $700 US. That meant I would have to make three transfers over three days to total $2,000 US. And it would be demanding for Chava, too, because he would need to go to La Paz to collect the money. I decided to take the chance and give him the money before the work was complete.

"I would like to pay you what I owe, but you have to promise to finish all the work within the next two weeks," I tell him.

"Of course," he says. "You are my amigo."

I reach into my bag and hand him an envelope containing two thousand dollars.

"But two weeks. No excuses," I say.

"Si, we're almost finished," he says.

I say goodbye, get in the van with Emily, and drive to La Paz to begin our trip home. The house disappears in the rear view mirror. In a few months, I've bought a house and almost finished it. In the autumn, I would build a pergola over the upstairs deck, an outdoor kitchen, paint the house, and add the solar system. I was eager to decorate and then spend the season kiting and having parties. I fell in love with my Baja home and knew I would be pining for it all summer.

Stormy Weather

Thousands of yellow butterflies flicker over the highway at the pass to La Ventana. I slow so I don't kill any. It's stifling hot, and my windows are wide open. A butterfly flies into the van and lands on the dash. I pull over and put my hand next to it. The butterfly climbs onto a finger. I lift it outside, and it flies away. As I drop into the valley, the butterflies thin, and I speed up. Soon, I turn into the Cardon forest, and ten minutes later, I climb the hill to the house. I have been away for five months.

From the road, her grey walls jut out of the desert. As I pull up, I see a six-foot-high pile of garbage in the front yard; the bodega is unfinished and the house is as I left it, only worse because it's dirty.

I step out of the van and stand at the gate feeling flush. I walk past the pile of garbage. The litter has blown against the fence, and the yard looks unkempt. Stepping inside, the house is a mess. The kitchen is unfinished, with cinderblocks and half-used bags of cement on the floor. Chip bags, beer cans, and other garbage litter the room. The cement counters are smooth but cluttered with trash. One three-foot section of counter is colored dark green. Having one slab green and all the others grey looks peculiar. Chava had added pigment to the wet concrete.

The old table I bought on Facebook Marketplace, while I was in Canada, is in the dining area. It's eight feet long and cost $250 delivered from La Paz. Originally it had four planks and was too massive for the room. But David removed one of the middle pieces to make it more narrow. Both sides of the tabletop have irregular live edges and the slab is a couple of inches thick. The table is under protective sheets of plastic. A thick film of dust covers the sheeting, but I can glimpse the grain of the wood. The enormous mass of the table suits the room well. In the corner are two matching benches.

Along the wall is the cement couch. It isn't exactly what I had asked for but is acceptable. Its back is reclined and upholstered; it'll be fine, I think. I'm feeling a mixture of emotions, mostly rage.

I hear a car approaching and look outside. Chava parks his wife's beat-up sedan and gets out of the car.

"Compa," he calls.

"I'm fucking disappointed," I say.

"Si," he responds.

"You fucked me!" Chava looks down. "You lied to me."

"I went into the mountains last week with my shotgun. I wanted to kill myself," he says.

"I've had a lot of problems," he says. Chava then tells me about his depression and marital problems. For the next ten minutes, he tries to get me to pity him. I don't respond with much sympathy.

"I might still kill myself," he says.

"We all might kill ourselves," I reply.

During the summer, I had lots of time to reflect on my relationship with Chava. I had misjudged our friendship. This was my fault. He had seen an opportunity to exploit me. I had been gullible and naive. I now felt manipulated by his stories of suicide and depression. Feeling sorry for him was only making matters worse, I think. He doesn't need an enabler. I had already done that, and it had gone poorly for both of us.

"This is what we're going to do, Chava," I say. "Tomorrow morning, you're going to show up and finish my house."

"Si," he says. "I will see you in the morning." He walks back to the car.

I go upstairs and unlock the bedroom door. It's even worse than downstairs. Garbage is strewn in the corners, and there is a foul stench. My foam mattress is lying in the corner. The top sheet has the greasy outline of where Chava slept. He lived here for months and never laundered the sheet. Tequila bottles and beer cans are strewn everywhere. A desiccated mouse lays along one wall.

I walk back to the van and drive to a favourite beach. I park close to the water and look at the expanse. I empty one of my duffels and find a pair of board shorts. I change and walk into the sea—the warm water swallows my anxiety. I close my eyes in the stillness. For the next hour, I float and try to reconcile my frustration. As the sky darkens, I feel better.

I get out of the water and pull on a T-shirt at the van. I then walk to a restaurant a few hundred yards away. I sit at a table overlooking the beach and order a beer—the young waiter returns with a frosty bottle with a paper napkin around its neck. I have eaten here before. Without looking at the menu, I order Shrimp a la Diabla. The combination of a rich cream sauce with spicy jalapeños is always soothing. This restaurant wasn't the best, but they made this dish well.

As I sipped the beer, I felt grateful to be back. The Baja is one of the most beautiful places I've ever seen. The food is terrific and the people friendly and interesting. Chava had disappointed me. It was a setback, but everything would be back on track with a little hard work. When I finish eating, I pay my bill and head to the van. I unlock the top box and take my bedding from it. I unfold the rear seats and make my bed. I climb into the van and fall asleep.

In the darkness before dawn, I stumble to the water's edge. I sit with my feet in the sea. A meteor shower shimmers, and I breathe deeply with gratitude. Once the sun crests the distant mountains, the sky is bright, and I drive home.

Approaching my yard, my heart sinks upon seeing the pile of debris. I wonder how to approach the filth.

Instinctively, I get a bucket out and turn on a tap. But Chava used up my water long ago and didn't refill it. I go into the storage area under the outside stairs and get out several garbage bags. Like cleaning a dorm room after a party, I walk around the house picking up beer bottles and chip bags. I sweep up the dead mouse and find several others. I roll up my mattress with the high thread count sheets I had brought from Canada. I throw them onto the garbage pile in the yard.

I need to order a water delivery, but my phone isn't activated. So, I drive to the OXXO and deposit $15 into my account. I buy a big bottle of bleach and a bottle of pine-scented disinfectant. By the time I walk out of the store, I receive a text from Telcel saying my phone has data. While sitting in the van, I call the water delivery company. I go to Kijote Coffee since they're now open. The owner chats as she makes my Americano con Leche.

When I return to the house, it's already getting hot. I wander around the house, sipping my coffee. I make a list of everything I'll need for the next couple of days. When the water truck arrives, I already have a full page of tasks.

The water truck backs up, and a teen jumps from the cab. He uncoils a thick water hose and ties the end to a belt loop. Without hesitation, he scrambles up the ladder. A small gasoline water pump jumps to life beside the truck. Soon, I can hear the splash of the tanks getting filled. I hand the driver thirty bucks plus a tip and go inside to fill my bucket with detergent and water.

First, I add disinfectant to both toilets to soak as they are discoloured, and soiled. I fill another pail and start mopping the upstairs. The water is still opaque after two washings. The downstairs is less dirty and, after a single wash, is in decent shape. I scour the toilets again and clean the sinks. When Chava shows up, the house smells of pine.

"I'll tell you what I need you to do," I say without saying good morning.

"Si," he says.

"I need you to have the trash in the yard picked up right away."

"Si," he says.

"I still have cleaning to do, so I will stay inside," I tell him. "I need you to get my doors and windows delivered," I say.

"Si," and he takes out his phone and walks back to his car to start making his arrangements.

I'm on a cleaning roll. I fill my garbage bag with the trash I missed. I have garbage cans soaking with bleach water, and the toilets are ready for another scouring. A half-hour later, Chava steps inside.

"The doors will come tomorrow, and the kitchen window will come this afternoon," he says.

"What about the garbage?" I ask.

"Later today."

"Good," I say. "Now, I need you to finish the bodega."
"I need to rent a mixer," he says.

"Then get one; we have water for the concrete."

"Si," and he walks back to his car and drives away.

I am now his project manager, not his client. He owes me, and I'm not interested in excuses or chit-chat. I don't want to discuss his problems. I only want to get his projects finished so he can leave. Listening to his excuses isn't going to improve anything.

It feels good to see the house already looking better. By this point, my list is two pages long. The first page has a to-do list of incomplete Chava projects. The second is a column of supplies and equipment needed. I tape these lists to the wall. It feels good to have a plan.

While Chava is getting the mixer, I text Lucas that I'm back in town. I tell him I love the table and benches and ask for his help. Fifteen minutes later, he's in the yard. Lucas parks his rusty truck beside the van. He has a huge smile.

"I'm so happy to see you," I tell him.

"Welcome back," he says, giving me a fist bump.

"I spent the morning cleaning," I tell him.

"It was filthy before," he says.

"I didn't know Chava was living here," I explain.

"He has muchos problemas," Lucas says.

"Yes, but they are his problems," I say. "He's going to work on some things, which I hope he can finish."

"Maybe he will," said Lucas, smiling. I had never heard Lucas disparage anybody.

"I need you to help me with some things," I tell him.

"I will help in any way I can," he says.

We step inside and look at the list on the wall.
"I wrote this list this morning,"

"Bueno," says Lucas.

I read out each item, and if he can help, I write a "L" next to the item. When we reach something he can't do, he usually says he knows somebody who can. Soon my house will be back on track.

"What would you like me to do first?" asks Lucas.

"I would like the kitchen finished so I can make coffee," I tell him.

"Why is this one green?" he asks, pointing to the counter beside where the stove will go.

"I don't know, but I hate it," I reply.

"To make it grey, a mason will need to chisel the top and re-pour concrete."

"Is that a big job?"

"A couple of hours to get rid of the green and then pour concrete," he says.

"Then I will need him to put on the backsplash mosaicos tiles I bought last spring," I explain.

"Your kitchen will be beautiful," says Lucas. He always redirects the conversation to the bigger picture. This is one of the best parts of working with Lucas. He is hopeful.

Lucas makes his list in a notepad. Using an old tape measure, he plans the cabinet doors, a spice rack, and a bunch of other things. I tell him I don't want pine because the termites will devour it. I want all of the wood to be parota to match the dining room table and benches. He agrees. By the time Chava returns, we have a detailed plan.

Lucas greets Chava. They speak between themselves for ten minutes. I strip the bathroom floors and wall tiles a third time. For the rest of the day, Chava arranges cinderblocks for the bodega. In the afternoon, a couple of men arrive and install the kitchen window. Its black frame makes the kitchen look more finished. A truck shows up later and hauls away the garbage pile. By late afternoon, the house is looking less grim. When Chava leaves, I go back to the beach for a long swim and a second meal of Shrimp a la Diabla. Since my bed in the van is still made, I camp a second night on the beach.

Five men with a truckload of logs and sticks arrive one morning. They're building a pergola on the deck upstairs. I move the deck furniture into the bedroom as they lift the wood from the yard onto the deck. These guys don't mess around and get to work.

They attach four posts to the inside wall of the deck using long bolts. They climb ladders and attach beams using long wooden pegs. It reminds me of once watching Mennonites build a post-and-beam barn. They tie other beams using quarter-inch hemp ropes. The hemp lays in decorative and strong wraps.

After a couple of days, the frame is strong and secure. It can flex in a hurricane, but in anything less, it's robust. Finally, they place bundles of quarter-inch-thick sticks on the deck. These will be bent into the spaces between the beams to provide shade.

"We cut them in the full moon," one of the workers tells me.

I have never considered the importance of the lunar cycle when harvesting a tree.

"They're Palo de Arco and very strong," he says.

Clearly, I'm out of my element in this conversation. These workers have carefully selected every piece of wood for the pergola. They had even cut the wood on the one night of the month they felt was optimum. Using hand saws, they carefully cut the branches and bend them tightly together without using glue, nails, or rope. I'm not sure why they're doing what they're doing. But the results speak for themselves. Soon, I had a custom pergola in the ancestral tradition of Baja. On the full moon, it allows the deck to be illuminated. During the day, it creates a shaded spot to read or visit with friends. I couldn't be more thrilled.

After another dreamy sunrise, I drive to La Paz. The first stop is the ATM to give Lucas money for supplies. I also need to get a new mattress from Walmart and other supplies. When I get back to the house in the early afternoon, the two exterior wood doors are installed. The rich grain and thickness of the wood makes them feel stately and secure.

"They look good," I say to Chava.

"My uncle made them," he says.

"Aren't they supposed to have a finish?" I ask.

"We didn't know what you wanted, so we left them unfinished," he replies.

This is a cop-out because he could have asked. In the desert, having anything unfinished is all kinds of wrong. While the doors are beautiful, structurally, I can see they are not what they need to be. Lucas will need to rebuild and refinish them. Grateful to have the doors on site, I carry a bag of groceries to the kitchen counter. I walk to the wall and add "Finish exterior doors" to Lucas's list.

An hour later, a man and his young son show up with Lucas. He is a mason and has a three-pound hammer and a spike. For the next couple of hours, he chips the green countertop until it is roughened. He fastens a thin border of plywood to the edge of the counter while his son mixes fine concrete in a bucket. The mason trowels the concrete until it's smooth and has a glassy finish. Chava comes into the kitchen and examines his work.

"I want all the countertops to match," I tell him.

"I liked it the way it was," Chava says.

"I like things to match," I say.

I remember Chava once saying that gringos have boring taste. I change the subject and ask about his SUV. This is the first personal thing we have discussed since I returned.

"The transmission broke, and it was too expensive to fix," he says.

"That's too bad."

"Now I have to borrow my wife's car, and when she doesn't let me use it, I have to drive a dirt bike," he says.

"At least you don't have to travel far," I reply.

"Life is crazy," he says, shaking his head.

We go back to work for another hour. Already, we seem to be mending our relationship a little. Seeing progress is good for us. The walls of the bodega are now six feet tall, and soon, he will pour the concrete roof. I get out my level, and the walls are plumb. I go for a swim.

I return in the dark and make a sandwich. I go upstairs and set up the air mattress I bought at Walmart. It has a flocking top, and when covered with a sheet, it is surprisingly comfortable.

I'm going back to Los Angeles in about a month and sailing a friend's boat to La Paz. Since the boat has plenty of storage, I plan to pick up a high-density foam mattress then.

The following day, the mason and his son remove the plywood from the counter. It's smooth and looks terraced. They fill the screw holes that held the plywood in place. They lay out a row of mosaicos on the counter and then start mortaring them in place. When they get to a corner, they cut the tile free hand with an angle grinder. A couple of hours later, they've finishing off the grouting. The blue and white starburst mosaicos make the grey concrete countertops pop.

"Very beautiful," says the mason. His son nods in agreement.

Chava brings in a few men to finish the walls of the bodega and add the ceiling. It's the same process as when they built the addition. It's ridiculous that all this work wasn't done then. In the afternoon, I brave the desert heat and returned to the ATM. Lucas's work is going to add up quickly.

After going to the bank, I pass a music store. I've been listening to a local Cumbia radio station and I'm crazy about it. Cumbia is a popular dance music that has spread across Latin America. While I'm familiar with the music, they never seem to introduce the music in Mexico. As a result, I don't know the names of any songs or bands. I want to have my own collection of Cumbia that I can keep on my phone and listen to back in Canada. The store is filled with racks of CDs. I go to the Cumbia section and don't recognize any of it. The clerk asks if he can help me.

"I like Cumbia," I say.

"Which bands?" he asks.

"I don't know," I say feebly.

He smiles and leads me to his computer at the back of the store. He explains he can sell me a huge collection of MP3s. He taps on the keyboard and a list of Cumbia titles appears. He says he can sell me a 16 GB flash drive and will copy the music onto it.

"That would be great," I tell him. He takes a USB thumb drive off a hook on the wall and opens its packaging. He plugs it into his computer and with a keystroke is copying thousands of songs onto it.

"If you listen to Cumbia, you need to have a light," he says. "It makes the music better."

I must have looked confused because he leads me to the front of the store. He lifts a box off a shelf and puts it on the counter. It's what we call a disco light back home. A five-inch-round plastic light. Colourful LEDs spin inside and project on the wall. I laugh at this suggestion and say why not?

He taps into his cash register, and I pay him $7 for the thumb drive and $7 for the Cumbia light. It reminds me of my first car. I bought a 1971 Volkswagen van after college for $600. I then bought a $600 stereo, explaining to the clerk it would be wrong to have a stereo that cost more than the vehicle it was in. A few minutes later, the download is complete and I head home.

When I return, I stop by Lucas's store. He never has much inventory. He does quality work, and I assume things sell fast. He shows me an estimate for the things I asked him to do. Cabinet doors, spice rack, plywood shelving in my bedroom, and several smaller items. Everything is in order, and I gladly give him a deposit.

At the house, I load thousands of songs onto my computer and then onto my phone. Finally, I can see the names of bands and tracks. I learn my favourite Cumbia bands are Grupo Canaveral and La Sonora Dinamita. I also discover new favourites not played on the radio. And the salesman is right. Cumbia does sound better with a flashing light.

Lucas stops by later to check his measurements for the kitchen. Cumbia is blaring and the light is flashing. I'm listening to the song Mi CuCu by La Sonora Dinamita. I assume it's about the bird. Lucas patiently explains it's about the gauze-like wraps women use to cover their bikinis at the beach. I laugh at my simplistic ignorance.

I ask Lucas to consider building me a bed. I explain I want something rustic. I tell him that I love the pergola and wonder if I could have a bed made similarly.

"That could be very beautiful, or it could be very ugly," he says.

"Let's hope for very beautiful," I say.

"I need to talk to the carpenter to find out how to build it," he says.

"In the meantime, please concentrate on the kitchen and the storage shelves in the bedroom," I say.

"Of course," he smiles.

The afternoon drive was too hot for me. I'm uncomfortable and need to cool off. I guzzle an electrolyte drink and explain to Lucas I need to go for a swim. He looks at me sympathetically. He can see I'm flush and lethargic. I tell Chava that I'll be back later. I plunge into the water and feel instant relief. When I return an hour later, Chava and his guys are gone. The walls of the bodega are finished, and the matrix of rebar is positioned for the pour. An array of 2 x 4s supports plywood from below and styrofoam blocks are in position on the roof.

The next day, Chava shows up mid-morning without his wife's car. At noon, I bring him a cold lemonade. He's working at half speed and has a pained expression on his face. Having him work at half-speed is better than him not working at all, I reason.

"I need special screws for the bodega," he says.

"Tell me what you need, and I will go to the hardware store," I reply.

"I can go myself."

"It's better you work here," I say.

"I need $10 for supplies," he repeats.

"I will drive you to the hardware store," I say.

"I'm a rancher, and I need to walk. A gringo wouldn't understand that," he says.

I resent the way he calls me a "gringo." It's an insult. I'm getting fed up with him and hand him $10.

"Come right back," I say.

Chava disappears down the road. I text him, but he never answers. I put away his tools and lock them in the storage area under the stairs. I don't see Chava again until the following morning. He walks into the yard and starts working right away.

"What happened yesterday?" I ask from the upstairs landing.

"The hardware store didn't have my supplies, so there wasn't any point coming back," he says without looking up.

"I will never give you money again," I tell him.

He shrugs his shoulders.

A couple of his helpers arrive and, after a few days of unfocused work, put the roof on the bodega. Chava is not engaged and sometimes disappears for hours at a time.

It will take him forever to finish at this rate, I think.

One morning, I get a text from a friend saying that a big storm is coming. I haven't been following the weather reports but I know we are still in hurricane season. I check my weather app, and the next few days will have high winds and lots of rain. While this won't be a hurricane, the storm will pack a wallop. I'd never seen a big storm in the Baja.

I start preparing. I bring all my deck furniture inside my bedroom. I load all my tools into the storage area under the stairs. I bring the garbage cans into the kitchen to not blow away. I don't have many belongings and within half an hour I'm in good shape. I do my dishes and organize some clutter.

The day is quiet and still. In town, people screw sheets of plywood over windows. Steel hurricane shutters are everywhere as the town buttons up. These people know the drill.

The setting sun illuminates a curtain of the darkest clouds I have ever seen. Within an hour, the shriek of gusts against my ladder fills my head like a dentist's drill. I watch the stout pergola twist, and the first of its sticks dislodges and falls onto the deck. Sheets of rain pound everything. The drops are thick and heavy. Lightning cracks in wide, strobing bursts. It's all-consuming, and I stand at my bedroom window hypnotized by the ferocity of the storm.

I run downstairs and get drenched. The rain is heavier than a bathroom shower. I open the door with both hands, fearing it will be ripped from my grip. I look around the room, and everything is dry. Getting back to the bedroom, I change my drenched T-shirt, vowing to go shirtless next time.

The wind and rain only get heavier. Sheets splash in the disorganized gusts—the deck fills with water. Chava neglected to drill any drainage.

"Fuck!" I yell into the storm. An inch-deep pool is already on the deck.

Water is shooting off the roof from two gutters above the deck. The cinderblock walls of the deck form a swimming pool of water and threatening to run into the bedroom. I move my clothes into the shower stall to keep them from getting wet. I roll up towels and place them against the sliding doors. Every ten minutes or so, I mop the puddles that form. I run back downstairs, and there are puddles under both doors. There is also a puddle against the back wall even though there isn't any openings on that side of the room. I mop the puddles and then run upstairs and mop my bedroom.

But what concerns me most is the water accumulating on the upstairs deck. Before it can breach the two-inch lip protecting the bedroom, I intervene. I strip to my underwear and step outside with a bucket. The water level reaches my ankles. In the blasting wind, I start bailing. Bucket after bucket, I'm bailing slightly faster than the water accumulates. After a while, the water level starts to drop. After an hour, the water level is down an inch.

"Fucking Chava!" I yell into the storm. I had been after him for weeks to add drainage.

"Don't worry," he said. I had forgotten to check that the work was done.

I take a break and mop the bedroom, and then run downstairs. The puddle from the stove now covers half the room. I mop and then run back to the deck to bail. After almost three hours of frantic effort, the rain softens. I mop more leisurely and bail the deck to less than an inch of depth. In the darkness of a flashlight, I towel off, dry my hair, and eat a peanut butter sandwich that I wash down with a beer.

At six, I text Chava that he neglected to install a drain. I need him to come over right away. He texts back, promising to be over as soon as he can. The road is out and getting to La Ventana will be tough. I go back to the deck and bail, but my back starts to spasm.

With daybreak, the rain stops. The morning light makes the stucco steam. I open every door and window. I get in the van and drive into town. Several trees lay across the roads, and I drive a circuitous route. The arroyos are massive brown torrents, and debris litters the beach. The sodden ground is unable to support them in the wind. I go home, lay on my air mattress, and sleep.

Chava shows up at five. He carries a small sledgehammer and a spike. He holds the spike against the cinderblock of the deck's wall. After twenty blows, a stream of water pours off the deck. He enlarges the hole, and soon only puddles remain.

"I asked you several times to add a drain," I say.

"Si," he says.

"You must do better," I say. Chava doesn't say anything and leaves.

The next day, I drive to La Paz and buy a kitchen stove. On my way back, I drive a road I have never been on. I'm driving a little fast but not crazy fast. I see a tope, or speed bump, on the road. I don't have time to slow down. The van hits this one especially hard. My head jams against the roof. The collision is loud and the stove crashes on the plywood bench. I pull over and turn off the engine. I walk around the van and near the tope notice a piece of spring.

Is that mine? I wonder.

I pick up the curl of metal and look under the van.

Instead of putting up speed limit signs, they build topes. These speed bumps come in varying sizes and are always better than epot's. An epot is a trench that can tear the undercarriage off a car. Epot is tope backwards. When they paint lines on the road to look like topes they're called "faux-pes."

Before getting back in the van, I search for a shop specializing in suspensions. Soon Google Maps has brought me to a shop a few miles away. I walk into the office and ask if someone can look at the van. A mechanic wearing navy coveralls comes outside and I show him the spring.

"Pinche tope," I say.

He laughs and climbs under the rear of the van. After five minutes, he tells me that I have broken a spring. He phones someone and, in a few minutes, tells me there is a wrecker that has a replacement spring. For $100 I can have the replacement installed. I'm getting off easy.

Soon, a teen on a dirt bike arrives. I give him money for the part and he's back in ten minutes. The van is already in the lift and the broken old spring is being removed. Ten minutes later, I'm back on the road as good as new. I promise myself that I will slow down and be more careful. But it's a half-hearted promise.

When I get home, I call Lucas and tell him that I have a kitchen stove. Later, a propane guy installs a tank and runs a fuel line to the stove. I can now make coffee and cook. I move my cooler into the kitchen, and every couple of days empty water and fill it with ice. It's crude, but it keeps my coffee cream from spoiling, and there is always a cold beer in the afternoon.

Chava is working alone, and he asks me to get some wire at the hardware store. It isn't my cost as I have already paid for supplies. But I want to get the house finished. I drive to the hardware store and stop by the coffee shop, where I bump into a couple of friends and have a cortado. When I get back to the house, Chava is gone. An hour later, I open the cooler to make a sandwich and notice that all my beer is also gone. In the yard are nine empty beer cans. Chava is probably sleeping it off in Arroyo somewhere.

In the morning, he gets to work late. He isn't talking much, so I broach the elephant in the room.

"I didn't offer you a beer," I say.

Chava doesn't look up from his work.

"Leave my shit alone," I yell, but he doesn't engage.

A couple of days later, Chava asks me to go to the hardware store for nails. I drive down to the hardware store and again get a cortado and check my email. When I return forty-five minutes later, he's gone. I walk to my bedroom, and everything seems in order, though my clothes are rumpled. I had a half bottle of tequila hidden under t-shirts in the back. The tequila is gone. I walk onto the deck to see if I can see Chava anywhere. On the other side of the fence, I can see the glint of the empty tequila bottle. Immediately, I start moving anything of value into the van.

"This guy has no shame," I mutter.

Late the next morning, he arrives at the house, smiling and singing a ballad. I walk downstairs to confront him.

"I don't appreciate you stealing my booze," I say.

"Si," he replies, busying himself.

"You went through my things," I yell. Chava shrugs but doesn't say anything and organizes tools.

A couple of hours later, I drive to town to do a video chat for work. When I return, Chava is sitting in the shade of the house. I'm fighting a losing battle.

"You're keeping your booze locked in your van," he says.

"Of course. Otherwise, you would drink it all."

"I can't control myself," he yells at me.

"That's because you're an alcoholic." Our eyes meet. "You need treatment."

He stands up, and I think we might fight. He starts arranging some boards he used for stucco. I go upstairs and have a shower. By the time I'm dressed, he's gone. I know he won't be back.

I text Lucas and tell him I need his help. There is still a window missing. And mice are coming inside my house every night. The bodega door still hasn't arrived, and I need to be able to lock my kiteboards and bicycle or they will be stolen. There are several other things that Chava has been paid to supply that are missing.

Lucas lines up tradesmen. Within hours, there is a window guy taking measurements. A welder builds a locking door for the bodega that is stout and fits with the rough-hewn look of the house. Soon, painters give an estimate. It's refreshing to be working with new faces. I feel hopeful that I've turned a corner.

I don't blame Chava for taking advantage. I was being careless, and it was more embarrassing than anything else. In a way, I deserved what I got for being gullible. That lesson cost me a little cash and some frustration, but it's well learned. My dealings after he quits improve. I start giving tradesmen a minimal deposit. I'm much more clear about expectations and deadlines. I play the role of "El Jefe." The workers seem comfortable with this clear delineation. And so am I. It's a simpler and less confusing way to work. I learn I can still be kind, but I need to stop being a schmuck.

That evening, I drive to the nearby boat launch of Ensenada Muertos, where there is a small restaurant. Nestled into a cove below a protective hillside, the restaurant is open air and has a palapa roof. Fishermen have used this harbour for millennia. I always order the Shrimp Chiles Rellenos here. They are a pepper filled with shrimp and fried in a light batter. When prepared correctly, they are irresistible.

I'm relieved not to be working with Chava and finally making progress again, but I miss Chava. I enjoyed his stories and the way he explained life in Baja. And I am glad to be working with different people.

After I place my order and have a frosty beer beading on the table, I send my friend Stephen Kelemen an email. Stephen is a brilliant painter and has been a close friend for decades. His use of color in his art is sensitive and impactful. If anyone can help me choose colors, it would be Stephen. When my meal arrives, I watch the vibrancy of the setting sun and feel elated.

"I love Baja," I think while chewing the tender peppers.

As I lay in bed watching another magnificent sunrise, my phone hums. I fumble for my reading glasses. It's a message from Stephen. He suggests I look at the work of the great Mexican architect/designer Luis Barragan. Attached is a photo of a bright pink and purple courtyard from one of his houses. I know of Barragan and had once visited a building he designed in Mexico City. Barragan used color like no one else. Bright pinks, purples, and yellows screamed from his walls.

I study the photograph, and the simplicity and vibrancy wash over me. I had never considered what colors to paint my house. There always seemed to be more pressing issues. Besides, most middle-aged gringos like me play it safe. We tend to paint our houses shades of sand or terracotta. Barragan's colors are alive, festive, and very Mexican.

My mind made up, I pull on a pair of shorts and make a coffee in a go cup. I sip it as I drive to Home Depot in La Paz. I walk past the greeter directly to the paint section. I study paint chips at a wall display. I hold my phone up and look at the Barragan photograph. Within ten minutes, I have matched his colors. A clerk asks if I need help. I show him the picture on my phone and point to the color chips. He looks at me with confusion as if to say: "Are you out of your fucking mind?"

The bubble gum-coloured chip is more suited to a tween girl's bedroom. Behind it is a vibrant purple that also shouts for attention. I ask him if he thinks these chips are similar to those in the photo. It's difficult to color match from a photo on the phone. You aren't sure what time of the day the photo was taken or if the day was cloudy or the image color corrected. The clerk shrugs and doesn't say anything. I feel the Gods of Modernism smiling at me. I'm confident that the colors are what I want. While they may not be exactly Barragan's, they are in the spirit of Barragan. I'm okay with that.

The clerk takes me to an aisle with rows of paints in five-gallon pails. I ask for a high-quality imported paint I've used back home. He cautions that what I want is very expensive. Most Mexican's buy cheap paint that only lasts 2-3 years. Having a house painted in Mexico is inexpensive, so why not paint more often? I explain that I want a ten-year paint. I ask for seven five-gallon buckets of a bright white, one drum of pink, and one of purple.

The clerk leads me to the paint counter, creates a receipt on a computer, and hands me a copy. I walk to the front of the store and stand in line. When it's my turn, I pay for the paint and return with the receipt. The clerk loads the paint onto a couple of trollies with a helper. The white paint goes into an agitator for mixing. The buckets that are going to be pink and purple are brought to a mixing station. The clerk looks at me and says, "Are you sure?" He's trying to give me a way out.

"Yes, I love Luis Barragan," I say with exuberance.

On the drive home, I realize that the clerk likely doesn't know who Luis Barragan is. He probably thought I was confessing my love for a boyfriend named Luis.

He shrugs his shoulders and prepares the paints. Before squeezing the pigments into the paint, he looks at me.

"Are you sure?" giving me another out. I nod. "Yes."

Bright pink pigment the consistency of toothpaste squeezes into the bucket. The clerk sighs as if to say, "they don't pay me enough for this shit." He puts the lid on the bucket and slides it into the agitator.

"It will be ready in fifteen minutes," he tells me.

I thank him and walk over to the garden center to consider plants.

The painters show up the next day. They are friendly guys in their twenties. They lay out a couple of ladders in the sand in the yard. They position long telescoping poles, trays, rollers, and brushes. Standing back, they take a moment to ensure they have everything they need.

They open a bucket of primer and fill the roller trays. Using rollers on long poles, they reach much of the second-floor walls. By early afternoon, they have covered most of the house. They are now on ladders with brushes, cutting in around the edges. By the end of the day, they have primed the house without hardly spilling a drop. These guys are serious.

The following day, they arrive at 8 a.m. They carry the bucket of pink paint to the north wall. They pull off the lid, and we gasp at the vibrant sheen. I had warned them that I was painting that bright wall pink. Nothing I could have said would have prepared them for the intensity of that hue. Both men laugh. They know who Luis Barragan is and seem to appreciate that I'm trying to honour him.

"Chingon," says the older painter with a smile. I feel they understand what I'm attempting. At the same time, they might have thought they'll be hired to cover up the pink later in the week.

They roll thick coats of pink, and immediately the wall comes to life. Since it's in shadow all day, the vibrancy of the hue is a little subdued. And when the paint dries, I feel it will tone down a little more. I look at the color from various distances and angles without saying anything.

"Es bueno?" the painter asks.

"Muy bonita," I reply, smiling.

A couple of hours later, the first coat is complete. I can't resist watching the paint dry. It gives the angles of the house greater definition and makes it appear more "architectural." Pride wells in me, and I hold up the photo Stephen sent in comparison. I take a single picture and send it to Stephen. A few minutes later, he responds with a single word: "Amazing!"

I meet friends at a taco truck called "Baja Bites" for Lunch. Kim and Claudia live on a sailboat in La Paz. Kim, a retired university professor, is knock-you-on-your-ass smart.

Claudia, a Columbiana, has an irresistible spirit and could break out in a song or dance at any time. They are two of my favourite people.

They've brought an Italian woman named Piera who they met at the laundromat. She's in her mid-thirties and has an art background from the University of Siena. She wears large silver bracelets and a heavy necklace of radiating metal, which sets off her olive skin. Piera has spent a year on an art pilgrimage through Mexico. When she saw the Two Frida's, Frida Kahlo's seminal work, it made her cry. She has studied murals by Rivera and others. She understands the historical context of art in Mexico.

As is always the case at Baja Bites, the tacos are shockingly good. They are fresh and perfectly prepared with simple dressings of the highest quality. And these tacos are transcendent. After lunch, my friends ask to see the pinkness of my house. For the first time, it occurs to me that people will now refer to my house as the "pink house."

Piera jumps in the van, and Kim and Claudia follow in their small rental. We make small talk, and soon my pink house is screaming on the horizon. Kim and Claudia pull up behind and get out.

"That's something," says Kim.

They laugh at the boldness of the paint. Piera doesn't say a word, and I feel self-conscious. She walks up the drying wall and leans towards it.

"It's beautiful; I love it," she says, touching the wall.

I'm elated that such a fashionable woman approves. Piera speaks to the painters, praising their work and telling them she loves the colors. "It's perfect," she repeats over and over. We go upstairs for a beer in the shade of the pergola.

For the first time, I feel a strong sense of pride. The house exceeds expectations, and those long days fighting Chava are fading. I can see the finish line, and it's time to start having more fun.

Cockblocked by Buddha

Waiting for tradesmen is a daily reality. After a coffee, I usually watch the sunrise, tidy up the house, and have a shower. I go to Kijote Coffee most mornings to send emails, visit friends, or video chat with my kids. Most tradesmen rarely show up at my house before ten anyways.

When work is being done, I try to be at the house most of the time. Not to supervise, but to answer questions. I often make the tradesmen coffee, lunches, or treats. Sometimes in the afternoon, I give them light beer. The workers wear boots, jeans, and long sleeve shirts. I never understand how they can stand the withering heat heavily dressed.

"So hot!" they exclaim, wiping their brows and taking a swig of Coke. These guys are tough.

In the afternoon, I pick up a friend to go for a swim. As we drive along the main drag, a woman walks her dog and waves.

"Who's that?" asks Tom.

"That's Sarah," I reply.

"She's gorgeous," he says. "You should ask her out."

"She's my meditation teacher," I explain. He looks at me like I'm crazy.

"Plus, she has this whole Buddhist practice. I don't think she even dates," I say, knowing deep down that even if she were dating, she would be way out of my league.

"Dude, you're getting cockblocked by Buddha!" he says.

This comment strikes me as particularly hilarious.

"Yeah, and have you seen that guy?" I say. "He never goes to the gym and is deep into carbs."

Tom nods in agreement.

"I could see losing out to Jesus. When you see him on the cross, he's ripped," I say

"But Buddha looks like a chubby baby."

"Totally," says Tom, shaking his head. We turn down a side street and park close to the beach.

In the morning, I notice a dark spot on the outside wall of my bedroom bathroom. I go upstairs and open the vanity. I remove the various cleansers and ephemera and see a discolored patch. I call Lucas, and in half an hour, a chubby plumber named Abel shows up with him. They look at the wall for a couple of minutes.

"Abel says we have to open up the wall to fix the pipe," says Lucas.

"That sounds like a big deal," I reply.

"It'll take a couple of days and will cost less than a few hundred dollars," he says.

Repairs in Mexico always seem inexpensive. I learn how easy it is to open up a cinderblock wall with a sledgehammer and fix a PVC pipe. The plumbing is part of the old house. I'm curious to see what is inside my walls.

The following day, Abel arrives early with his teenage son. They climb to the roof and turn off the water at the tanks. They disconnect the bathroom sink and remove the vanity that is bolted to the wall. They then start beating the walls and floor with a sledge hammer. Within half an hour, I have a massive cavity in my wall and can now see into my bathroom from the yard. Abel steps onto the landing and asks me to come upstairs. I head to the little bathroom, and he leans down and pulls two pipes apart.

"No glue," he states matter-of-factly.

Somehow, the builders had forgotten to glue the pipes together. Over time, they've pulled apart and water is leaking into the wall. I'm relieved it's such an obvious problem. But walking away, I start to wonder about the construction quality in other areas of the house.

If you can forget to glue your pipes together, what else are you forgetting?

I have a three-foot hole in my floor and wall, and the amount of dust and dirt in my bedroom is shocking. Abel goes to the hardware store for supplies while his son fills a garbage can with broken bits of cinderblock and tile. When he returns, Abel sands the ends of the PVC pipe and glues them together. They then start to repair the massive hole in the wall and floor. His son climbs a ladder and screws a piece of plywood to conceal the cavity—Abel mixes mortar in a bucket. He trowels the mortar into the gaping hole. They attach more plywood to the inside of the bathroom wall. Soon, they are cleaning and putting away their few tools.

After they leave, I examine their repairs, and it dawns on me that several tiles need to be replaced.

"Should I get replacements in La Paz," I ask Lucas. "I'm going into town tomorrow anyway."

"Let me ask Abel," he says, hanging up.

A few minutes later, Lucas calls to tell me that Abel can get the same tiles in La Ventana and not to worry. Satisfied with all the progress, I go swimming and have dinner in town.

In the morning, I drive to La Paz before Abel and his son arrive. I run errands and go to the ATM. After stopping for lunch at Taco Fish, I'm back at the house by early afternoon. They're cleaning up when I arrive. I look at the house from the yard. Where the hole had been is fresh stucco drying in the sun. It looks great. All it needs is a little paint, which I will do myself. I go to the bathroom and on the floor are seven new floor tiles. They're a different shade and pattern from the tiles that were there originally.

"I thought you had the same floor tiles," I say to Abel.

"Similar, but different," he says.

I understand that this repair is acceptable to Abel. It's functional, and my pipes are now working. I'm okay with that.

Every night I continue to kill scorpions in my yard. While things have improved since I got my black light flashlight, they continue to wander to the house. For the first time, I wish I had a chicken. They love eating scorpions. Can I rent or borrow one? I wonder. I want to avoid hiring an exterminator to fog the desert with pesticides like many do.

I tell Lucas about my struggles and he suggests clearing the underbrush from the yard. It's overgrown and he says I have too much habitat for them. Scorpions live under sticks and leaves and burrow in the sand, he explains.

A few days later he brings a family of five to the house. They are dressed in long pants and long-sleeved shirts and wear leather gloves. They slash at the brush with machetes and collect tall piles of sticks and branches. When my yard is somewhat denuded, they work the adjacent lots beside my house.

After a couple of hours, I go to Star Market. I pick-up an assortment of cold drinks and treats. They are a husband and wife and an uncle, I think. Two teenage boys chase each other with boundless energy. A couple of hours later, a truck is hauling away a massive pile held down with thick nylon straps.

"You won't have scorpions or snakes now," the father tells me.

"I hope so," I say.

"It wasn't safe and now it is," he says, looking at my somewhat barren yard.

That night, I kill a scorpion on the fence. I continue my nightly patrols and am pleased the problem is improved.

I stand on my deck and watch the sunrise. The winds are already building. The mornings that were a little windy would often build into howlers by afternoon. Most days in La Ventana have at least some wind. That's why kiteboarders and windsurfers congregate here. If they come for two weeks, they can bank on a dozen days of kiting.

Storms called "Norte's" regularly blast the Sea of Cortez. They come from Texas in five-day cycles of cold, windy weather. They are dreaded by fishermen, but sailors and kiteboarders dream of these conditions. When the waves get big, they're "buffalos," and when they get really big, "elephants." La Ventana's unique geography only increases the wind speeds. Isla Cerralvo, eight miles away, funnels the wind and creates a natural wind tunnel.

I notice that the desert insects and birds seemed to "surge." This morning is a surge day. The low bushes and trees in my yard are full of birds hopping from branch to branch. I can see a couple of crimson-colored cardinals, several cactus wrens, and my favorite, a caracara, from my deck. A roadrunner sprints through a clearing, and a pair of hawks wheel in the sky—a fantastic display of diversity and sheer volume of life. But many days, I will only see one or two birds. Some nights, I find a dozen or scorpions in my yard. And then for the next week, none. I don't understand why animals are more active one day than the next. But I learn to seize the moment and take long walks whenever life is surging.

Lucas stops by in the afternoon to touch base. I tell him that I need to go to the upholsterers before my sailing trip. I want to get couch cushions made, and we discuss options. I need an upholstered foam base and about a dozen pillows for the backrest. Lucas offers to come with me to La Paz. He knows a good upholsterer and where to buy the best fabric. It feels as though he doesn't trust me to choose the material myself. And for a good reason. He's an aesthetic man, and I know choosing the correct fabric matters. My sofa is almost 15 feet long and will have significant presence.

The following day I pick him up at his store. He has a go-cup of coffee, and we stop at the coffee shop for mine. Lucas always seems better organized than me. We drive into the back of La Paz. He directs me to a ramshackle uphol-stery shop with a large green sign over its front door. Inside, five men drape and stretch fabric over chairs and sofas. They work without much talk, and a stereo blasts Cumbia. I find their long-nosed pliers, small hammers, and fabric stretchers fascinating.

Lucas speaks to a heavy-set man. He scribbles the dimensions of my couch onto a piece of paper. He adds a column of numbers and hands it to me. I now know how much fabric we'll need.

We drive down the road to a two-story store named "Vanessa." A young, stylishly dressed woman greets us as we walk inside. Looking at me, she points to a display of Sunbrella at the side of the store. She assumes I'm reupholstering deck chairs or cushions for a boat. I feel embarrassed to look shabby in my shorts and T-shirt. Lucas explains we need fabric for an oversized couch in my living room. She laughs at her mistake and apologizes. She leads us on a tour of both floors of the massive store.

Hundreds of rolls of fabric vie for my attention. We climb a steep staircase to reach a remnants section on a cat-walk. It's a little overwhelming, and I tell Lucas I don't know where to start. She leads us back to the entrance and smiles. She can see my confusion, and she asks to see a picture of my living room. I take out my phone and find a few images of my couch and the view from the window.

"Very beautiful," she says.

She explains that I should keep a solid or less patterned fabric for the base. Many people tire of their upholstery when they buy something too loud, she explains. This makes sense to me. I tell her I want something that won't show stains, and she agrees.

Lucas shows her a photo of my backsplash.

"Mosaicos?" She asks.

"Yes," I say.

"But they are for the floor," she says.

"Yes, but they are stunning," and she nods in agreement.

She leads us to several bolts of fabric in the corner. She roots around for a few minutes, finally pulling out a textured solid blue fabric.

"It will match the Mosaicos," she says.

But it might be a little boring, I think.

"That is the type of fabric you want," says Lucas.

"It's like the ocean," she says, asking to see the photo from my window.

I hold up my phone.

"Next, you need sky," she says. She walks to the opposite side of the room. We follow her, and soon she is holding a roll of lighter blue fabric.

"Sky," she says, putting it next to the "Sea" fabric.

Then she walks the stairs to the catwalk. Lucas and I follow, and she pulls a bolt from a tall shelf. The fabric is a blue and white zig-zag pattern.

"This will be the waves," she says, smiling.

I would never have thought of this combination. It's a little on the nose, I think. But the combination tells a story, and I like that. I look at Lucas.

"It could be great," he says.

"You don't think it will be too busy," I ask the woman.

"Mostly, it will be the dark blue you'll see," she says. "The other fabrics are accents, and you can let them be bold."

What she says makes sense.

"Ok, let's do it," I say.

Lucas hands her the measurements.

"It will be lovely," she says, carrying the fabric to the front of the store. She lays it on a long table and measures. Using a pair of enormous scissors, she cuts the material and folds it neatly into a plastic bag and I pay her.

"La Ventana is wonderful; my boyfriend's family has a lot of land there," she says.

"A lot of new homes," Lucas says.

"Many people are coming here now," she says, handing me the material.

"You have been wonderful," I tell her.

"It's been my pleasure," she says as we leave the store.

We bring the fabric to the upholsterers. After giving them a deposit, they tell me to come back in a couple of weeks to pick up the cushions. I'm leaving the next day for my two-week sailing trip, so the timing is perfect. We go to Taco Fish for lunch. It's been a painless outing—another milestone.

Taco Fish is the best lunch in La Paz. Unlike Baja Bites, they deep fry their seafood. Like Baja Bites, Taco Fish has the good sense to have a menu with only a few items. They also let you dress the tacos yourself. They have all kinds of dressings and sauces, and it's terrific for a visitor to try new things. All the tables are stainless steel, and it's open-air and scrupulously clean. For these reasons, there's often a line to get in. We eat our tacos and return to La Ventana by early afternoon.

The following day, I drive to La Paz to catch a flight to Tijuana. I'm helping a friend bring his boat to La Paz. I will be sailing in a rally called the Baja Ha-Ha for a couple of weeks. I'm sad to leave my house but I'm looking forward to a break.

LOVE BITES

When we dock the boat at Marina Costa Baja in La Paz, I can't wait to get back to La Ventana. I walk to the parking lot and pick up the van. I return to the boat and pick up my stuff. I struggle under the awkwardness of a high-density foam mattress I bought from a chiropractor in Los Angeles. After a quick goodbye with my friends, I'm on the road.

I'm thrilled to see Lucas has completed all his tasks when I arrive. The parota kitchen cabinet doors look fabulous. The drawers close smoothly, and everything fits perfectly. The large spice rack is finished in a flat finish and looks great. I go upstairs and see my bed for the first time. It resembles the pergola with chunky round wood legs, and woven Palo de Arco sticks making the headboard. At the corner of the room are wide plywood shelves for clothes. I feel emotional seeing everything for the first time and sit down to take it in.

I unload the van and carry the mattress to the bed. I cut the plastic, and it gasps for air and expands to a queen size. I unwrap some high-thread-count sheets and make the bed. I lay down, amazed with its breadth and comfort.

"Chingon," I say to myself.

When it gets dark, I go into the yard to check on the scorpions. I fear they have come back and shine my black-light while walking with a can of Raid. Car headlights appear, and Chava drives towards the gate in his wife's sedan. Poking out of the backseat window is a Cardon.

"Compa," he says. I haven't seen him since he walked off the job because I was locking up my booze.

"You have my Cardon," I say.

"And a good one," he replies.

When I bought my house, nine coconut palms were in the yard. These palms were problematic. They grow quickly but need water year-round. So, when you're back home, you must hire people to water them. At the back of my yard is a thousand-litre water tank with a hose for this purpose. And you run the risk of somebody getting clocked by a falling coconut. I like coconut, but one a year satisfies my needs. Besides, I preferred the look of the natural desert.

I had made a deal with Chava to sell the coconut palms if he replaced them with Cardon cactus. He has many Cardon at his farm in Los Planes, but it's illegal to transplant them without authorization. So, he was moving them at night when he was unlikely to be stopped by police. Chava had sold the palms for $50 a plant and had made $450. I looked at the seven-foot cactus and knew precisely where it would go.

"Let me get my gloves," I say.

"I can handle this," he says, lifting the enormous plant from his car.

I get a shovel and start digging a hole beside the house. Chava hulks the cactus to the spot and says he has others he needs to pick up, and leaves. I dig until I have enough depth to bury the hooked root of the Cardon. I slide it into the hole and push it vertical. I hold it in place while pushing sand with my feet to cover the roots. Once filled, I stomp the ground to make sure it's secure. I fill a bucket and water it. I step back from the cactus and admire it from different angles. Chava is right, it is a great-looking Cardon.

He brings two smaller ones an hour later. I plant them around the yard to make them appear to have grown naturally. These are so much better than palm, I think.

One morning I break a molar, biting a mint. I look in the bathroom mirror and see a fang-shaped tooth. I must have swallowed the other half. Somehow, it didn't hurt. A friend who is a retired dentist had told me about a dentist on the Malecon. He had cutting-edge equipment called Cerac and could make crowns while you wait. I lock the house and drive to La Paz.

I walk into the dentist's office, and a receptionist guides me to an examination room. A thirty-something dentist comes into the room. He introduces himself and looks in my mouth.

"You've come to the right place," he says. "You need a root canal, a titanium post, and a crown."

I sigh.

"Don't worry, we can do it all today," he says.

I go to the waiting room, and a half an hour later, an endodontist arrives. He shakes my hand and invites me back into the examination room. With little talk, he freezes my jaw with a large syringe. While my mouth freezes, he lays out his tools. He turns on the TV that is mounted to the ceiling and plays a DVD. It's a travelogue of Canada's Rocky Mountains. There are scenes of Maligne Lake and the Banff Springs Hotel. A fly-over of Mount Rundle with its layered rock tilted upwards. He takes out his drill and removes the tooth's root. He seals the hole and epoxies a titanium post.

"We're done," he says, turning off the overhead light. I feel around with my tongue, and I sense the tiny post even though my tongue is numb.

"Come back in two hours," says the first dentist when I walk into the waiting room. "I'll make your crown, and we don't have to freeze your mouth because your tooth is now dead."

I walk along the Malecon and then to a cafe named Doce Cuarenta. I find a seat in the courtyard and order a coffee and an egg and avocado sandwich. Only soft foods today, I think. Since they have Wi-Fi, I download "The Big Lebowski" to my phone. After a long walk, I return to the dentist. He waves a camera on a wand around my mouth. His computer fills with black and white images of the fang with the post in it. I watch the annoying video of the Rockies for a second time.

"Once I get enough money, I want to go to places like that," he says.

"I live sort of near there," I say. Where I come from, being a thousand miles away is almost next door.

"It's gorgeous," he says.

"So is Baja," I reply.

He works on the computer for several minutes and then puts a cube of porcelain into a machine on the other side of the chair. The machine whirs, and a window lets me see tiny jets of water spraying the cube. I watch the jets gradually carve my replacement tooth. Twenty minutes later, the machine stops, and he takes the wet tooth from it.

"This is your new tooth," he says, holding it to my face. I open my mouth, and he puts it on the post.

"It's a good fit already," he says.

He holds a set of white cards of different shades against my mouth to color match. It reminds me of my Luis Barragan color matching.

"All my teeth are Cerac," he says, smiling. "I chose Hollywood White."

The dentist smiles, and his uniformly bright white teeth look fake. He chooses a less Hollywood White color to match my rapidly yellowing teeth. He then goes to a back room to paint the tooth.

"Soon, the tooth will be out of the kiln, and I can glue it in," he says, walking back to the receptionist.

Five minutes later, he fills the tooth with epoxy and places it on the post.

"Bite hard," he says.

I bite on a piece of carbon paper to check for high spots. After he grinds away a couple places, I bite down again.

"You're done," he says.

I'm surprised by the ease of the procedure. I go to the waiting room, where his receptionist has already prepared the bill. It costs four hundred dollars for the entire procedure. Back home, the same thing would have cost thousands. I promise myself to only suck hard candies in the future.

I want to buy a few planters for the roof of the bodega. They will be oversized to hold large cactus. In the morning, I go to a concrete fabricator in La Paz. He sells fountains, planters, washbasins, and headstones. The owner's son is a muscular twenty-year-old. I look at a few large semi-circular planters painted a rich terracotta. Luis Barragan sometimes used terracotta as an accent color. Each planter is a metre in diameter and the walls are a couple of inches thick. They are beasts and easily weighed a hundred pounds.

"What are you using them for?" he asks.

"Planters for cactus," I say. Without a word, he gets an extension cord. He plugs in a giant drill and makes a few drainage holes in each of them. He lifts one of the planters into the back of the van without making a grunt. I hand him the cash and tell him I will be back soon.

When I get home, I lean the old Vista Marina sign against the back of the van. I push the planter onto the board, and it slides to the ground. Leaving the planter in the yard, I return to La Paz and have the other two put in the back. After a quick lunch at Taco Fish, I'm home.

I call Lucas and tell him that I need help lifting the planters onto the roof of the bodega. By dinner, five guys from town arrive. Three lift from below, and two on the roof pull a rope. The planters are soon in position. We have a beer as the sunset splashes across the sky.

At sunrise, I fill a few five-gallon pails with 3/4 crushed gravel leftover from the concrete work. This makes an ideal base for drainage at the bottom of the planters. I collect many buckets of sand from the desert, and half fill the planters. Chava shows up after dark with three cactuses in his wife's car. They are a few feet tall and of different species. One has several strange arms while another almost looks like a Cardon. I put on my leather gloves and lift the cactus into the planters. I shovel more sand into the bucket by head-lamp. Soon all the planters are filled, and I water them until there are puddles on the roof of the bodega. Seeing them in place in the moonlight is fabulous. From the deck, they had the illusion of being two stories tall. The house is looking finished, so I plan my first party.

I decide to make a paella for ten friends. In many ways, paella is the perfect party food. It's fairly easy to prepare and I can get all the ingredients easily. I usually cook it on the BBQ and buy a bag mesquite charcoal. I have a new paella pan, which is a few feet in diameter and can make enough for a dozen. If I'm going to fuck-up, I'm going to fuck-up big. Since the pan is new, it needs to be seasoned. I put it on the stove and heat it with oil. It doesn't take long to start smoking and gain a glossy surface.

Paella is alchemy. The result is somehow much greater than the sum of its parts. This famous rice dish is a mainstay in Spain. The biggest challenge is getting the slightly burned crust known as the Socarrat. It's always a little hit and miss with me. I don't want to serve a tomato shrimp pilaf. But timing when to stop cooking always seems a mystery.

I busily cut vegetables and organize the ingredients into bowls. Olives stuffed with blue cheese and a cheese board are on the counter. I also have more regional fare with a big bowl of guacamole and Totopos, the thick corn chips that are a staple in Mexico.

As my guests arrive, I make screwdrivers. I have a pile of orange halves in front of the juice press. I squeeze three or four oranges over a couple of cubes of ice, add vodka, and stir. It's one of the best screwdrivers any of us have ever had. Could there be anything easier?

They sip their drinks and nibble the snacks. The conversation is about the gusty winds that afternoon. They wear their best Mexican hoodies and board shorts. All skilled kiteboarders. Some have raced motorcycles. Some have been competitive downhill ski racers. But now they get thrashed in the surf every day. They brave high winds and seek big air jumps. Routinely, they push themselves in punishing conditions. Some are in their 70s, but most are in their 50s and 60s. I'm proud to have such spirited friends.

The screwdrivers loosen everybody up—the talk is punctuated by lots of boisterous, full-throated laughter. I try to keep as many people helping as possible. The most significant task is deveining the kilo of shrimp. I have two ingenious deveining knives, which I show a couple how to use. With a single motion, these hooked knives cut the back of the shrimp, exposing its digestive tract. A quick rinse to remove the thready bowel and shell, and you're done. I head to the backyard where Dave is describing a nasty kiteboarding mishap. I pour lighter fluid onto the charcoal and drop a match; it bursts into a fireball. Dave hums Ride of the Valkyries from the famous napalm scene in Apocalypse Now. I don't pay him any notice and carry out the vegetables and lay them on a sawhorse beside the BBQ.

When the charcoal burns down, I heat the massive paella pan. You can't rush a good paella. You're working on its time. When the pan is hot, I pour a generous amount of olive oil. I raise the edge of the pan and swirl the olive oil. When I drop in the onion, it sizzles.

"Perfect," I say.

Seeing me fumbling around, Janice asks to stir. Since she's a professional chef, I know I'm in good hands and pass her the spatula. Dave brings me another screwdriver. I'm starting to have fun.

When the onions are browned, Janice adds the Spanish rice to toast it for a few minutes. Then she pours in the shrimp stock in tiny glugs every few minutes. The rice absorbs the stock and builds flavors in the pan. After most of the stock is gone, she adds several pinches of saffron. Then she adds sea salt and smoked paprika and the pan takes on an intense red hue. As it bubbles away, we prepare to add everything else. We arrange wedges of tomato, shrimp, green peas, and mussels artfully around the pan. Janice deftly wraps it in tin foil to let it work. But for how long? If you unwrap it early, you will have rice pilaf. Leave it too long, and the bottom will scorch. I tend to be an impatient cook, and Janice knows it. She laughs at me whenever I ask if she thinks it's ready.

"Almost," she smiles.

Janice knows what she's doing, and she is wise to keep fending off my insistence. Everybody is in the yard at this point. The paella takes much longer than I ever would have thought wise. I fear the bottom is pure char, but I trust Janice's expertise.

"It's time," she says definitively. I can't wait to get it off the BBQ. I carry the pan to a trivet on the dining room table. I take a breath and tear off the tinfoil. I dig a spoon into the center and feel the yield of the Socarrat. It's clear Janice has timed it perfectly. I take a deep breath and thank her.

As we sit down, Erin arrives at the door. She is with a Mexican woman with lively eyes named Carmen. Erin apologizes for being late, and everyone makes room for them by sliding down the benches. Carmen says she doesn't have to eat because she wasn't invited.

"We have loads," I reassure her.

I start plating paella and passing them around the table. It's festive with lots of lively conversation. The paella is spectacular. Everybody has seconds, and some thirds. When we're finished, I clear the table and put the plates next to the sink. Carmen comes into the kitchen and fills the sink with water.

"I'll wash up later," I tell her.

"I would feel better if you let me help," she says.

"Well, why don't we do them together."

I turn on the kettle for decaf while dropping plates into the soapy water. I add a capful of bleach, telling her that I prefer to make sure that everything is antiseptic. She laughs at my cautiousness.

"What was it like growing up in La Paz?" I ask her.

"It was much smaller then," she says.

She then tells me about being a single parent. She raised her three children without any help from her husband.

"I would make my kids sandwiches for their school lunches," she says. "I didn't have enough food for me to have a sandwich."

"That must have been very difficult," I say.

"I would take a bite from each of their sandwiches because I wouldn't have any food until night," she stops washing and looks at me. "I called them Love Bites."

"That's wonderful," I say.

"My kids still ask me to take Love Bites out of their sandwiches. But we have money now."

Carmen doesn't see herself as a victim. She has endured her share of struggles. I find her inspiring.

For dessert, I serve pitaya and coffee. This cactus fruit always dazzles me. It's basically the same as Dragon Fruit and grows wild in Baja. The guy I buy them from has cut all the spines off the fruit with wire snippers. They are bright red when sliced in half. The sweet flesh resembles a cross between a pear and a kiwi fruit. It is a refreshing, simple taste that is neither overpowering nor benign.

The dinner has been a great success. I loved every moment of it—the house made entertaining easy. Christmas is in a week, and I'm already planning a Paella Christmas Dinner.

WIGGLY MAN

In Baja, I learn to appreciate the complex flavors of tuna. My favorite grill is El Mesquite. They cook on mesquite with simple marinades. Everything is fresh and made to order. Their tuna is lightly grilled. The tuna gets grill marks while the inside is bright red and sometimes chilled. The rich, marbled flesh is irresistible. Their margaritas are sweetened with cane sugar, and they squeeze the limes at the bar. I go to El Mesquite weekly.

Sushi is popular in Baja, and fresh tuna is everywhere. Friends catch it and serve tuna thinly sliced with soy sauce dips. In Japan, fish destined for sushi is flash-frozen to kill parasites. In Baja, it's served fresh.

Midway through the winter, my stomach is often gurgling. It's always upset and often groans. After weeks of mild discomfort, I asked a couple of Mexican friends about it. They say I should take Vermox. Most locals take Vermox twice a year, they say. I Google it and learn that it's an anti-parasitic medicine. Vermox interferes with the parasites ability to metabolize sugar. They die in a day or so. It's an over-the-counter medication and available everywhere.

I go to the pharmacy and buy a package. As I walk to the van, I pop a tablet in my mouth. Within a couple of days, I no longer have a sore stomach. I hate the idea of having parasites. I go back to the pharmacy and buy several more boxes.

Christmas is a couple of nights later. I have a half dozen friends over for paella.

Unfortunately, Janice can't come, and the paella is less successful. After dessert and coffee, I put the packages of Vermox on the table and encourage my friends to take them. They all gave it a try, and their stomach problems clear up as well.

As much as I like Mexican food, sometimes I crave other things. Getting a good pizza in Baja can be challenging. There are a lot of traditional pizzas that we are accustomed to back home. But getting a delicious Neapolitan pizza is difficult. Probably the best pizza in Baja is at the El Triunfo Cafe.

I invite Piera for pizza there. She has strong opinions about pizza and worked many years at high-end restaurants in Siena, Italy. She once told me about going to a Pizza Hut in London and crying. We sit at a counter near the blazing oven so we can watch the pizza being made. The owner comes in and speaks to us. He's friendly, enormous, and looks like a biker. He explains how he built the wood-fired oven and taught his staff to make Pizza Margarita. He imported the best ingredients from Italy, including San Marzano tomatoes and the legendary 00 flour. People in the mountains make soft cheeses and grow their basil. The owner tells the cooks to make us a Pizza Neapolitan.

"We don't have a traditional Neapolitan on the menu," he says.

The cooks stretch the dough and spread a tomato sauce called Pasata. They dot the pizza with fresh cheese, a sprinkle of olive oil, and whole basil leaves. A pizza peel slides it into the oven, and the cook stands watching. We can see the cheese bubble. A couple of minutes later, the edges char, and the pizza is done. Simple and elegant.

"This pizza is the best," says Piera, chewing a mouthful.

I taste the pizza and stop to savor its complexity. We quickly wolf the entire thing and finish our beers. The owner returns.

"How was it?" he asks.

"You could go to Naples and teach a class," says Piera. This is the highest compliment she could give. He smiles and leaves.

Brian invites me to start New Year's Eve at North Arroyo Campground. About twenty-five people camp in this intermittent creek bed. It's a free campsite beside the main campground. A group of young guys have spent days gathering wood for a massive bonfire. They're veterans of Burning Man, and they called their effort "Burning Bush." Several years before, there was an annual party of this name in La Ventana. The brush pile is now fifteen feet tall.

After dinner, I drive to North Arroyo and park beside Brian's trailer. The brush is lit a few minutes later. The evening breeze fanning it into an impressive fireball. Flames lick the sky twenty feet high—the heat from the dry wood pushes the ring of onlookers back in all directions. Several people dance to a couple of Djembe drummers. For lack of a better word, it feels "tribal."

"Do you want some acid?" asks Brian. I hadn't done LSD since I was twenty.

"Sure," I say without thinking.

He passes me a little piece of blotter paper, and I put it on my tongue.

Thirty seconds later, I have second thoughts. I don't do acid. I'm not a drug guy, I say to myself. But it's too late; I've already swallowed it. I look into the fire and regret my impulsiveness. I know I have to go with it. I don't know what to do so I get a bottle of water out of the van. I watch the fire and visit with friends while the acid kicks in. The flames roar in the breeze. The logs shift and start to fall after an hour.

"Let's check out Delaneys," says Brian.

We walk to the main road and towards the resort. Delaney's holds the best New Years' Eve party every year. The owner was in jail for tax evasion. But his son ran it in his absence and had a reputation for hosting wild parties. By this point, I'm feeling the acid. The trailing headlights of passing cars make me feel stoned.

Delaney's has a large room on the second floor. When we arrive, a band is playing "Hotel California" to an empty room. We walk outside and around the building. The unmistakable thump, thump, thump of techno music makes my chest pound. A DJ stands behind a mixing board with a large screen between the palm trees. A dizzying light show is synced to the music projected on the screen. A bar lines the back of the compound, and a couple of hundred people dance under the starry sky. I make my way through the crowd before finding a short concrete wall to sit-on. I watch the dancing as the acid washes over me.

A man dancing twenty feet away catches my attention. His joints bend in ways I have never seen before. He appears wiggly. I'm mesmerized. It is one of the most beautiful dances I had ever seen.

After an hour, Brian finds me.

"How're you feeling?" he says.

"I can't stop watching Wiggly Man," I say, pointing.

"It's incredible," says Brian. I slide over so he can sit beside me.

We watch Wiggly Man bend and twist for a long time. His movements are hypnotic. The trancelike rhythms of the techno music pound in our heads. After the fireworks at midnight, the party starts to wind down.

"Let's go back to Burning Bush?" suggests Brian.

Since Wiggly Man has stopped dancing, I agree. We walk along the beach, watching the surf and the dazzling night sky. When we get back to Burning Bush, it's a big pile of embers and coals. Fifteen people dressed in heavy ponchos and sweaters sit in the sand. A few play guitar and Djembe. It's a fitting end to the night. We sit in the sand and feel the radiant warmth of the fire. I lay back in the sand to watch the stars. The cool evening fills my lungs. Soon, I'm fast asleep.

I wake after sunrise to pressure on my arms, legs, and chest. I open my eyes and see five very scruffy street dogs lying on me and against me for warmth. I shift my arms from underneath them. They lazily move off me. Pins and needles make my fingers tingle. The dogs get to their feet, stretch, and walk away down the beach. I stand up, chilled and disoriented. Burning Bush is reduced to smoldering embers. I step through the dune towards Brian's trailer. He's awake, and when he sees me, he steps outside.

"Let's get some breakfast?" he says.

"Sure," I say, fishing for the keys in my jacket. We get in the van and drive towards the main road. I stop abruptly. It's Wiggly Man out for a run. He's wearing shorts and a T-shirt. His gait is unmistakable.

"Wiggly Man!" I say, pointing as he passes in front. It occurs to me Wiggly Man has a disability of some sort. It's been a rough night.

Late the following afternoon, I go to Baja Joe's. It's one of the older bars in La Ventana and probably my favourite. It has lots of beer on tap and doesn't feel that touristy. You can't see the water from the bar but you're close to the beach. I like the atmosphere at Baja Joe's. It's always fun.

I walk into the compound and see that several tables already have people at them. A few are still wearing wet suits from kiteboarding and are wet. I've also kiteboarded here and tucked a couple of hundred pesos in my wetsuit for a beer afterwards.

I take a table along the side and sit on a concrete couch. I order an IPA from a passing server. Soon Brian joins me. I haven't seen him since the morning we saw Wiggly Man running. We talk about his truck problems. He has a faulty fuel pump, but it's located inside his fuel tank and is a mission to fix. Since the restaurant is setting up their taco bar, we beat the rush and go over. We dress a couple of tacos and a woman with a metal cash box takes our money. We return to our table and soon our friends arrive. We order more beer as the sky darkens.

The Mexican Weirdos start setting up their instruments on the stage. It's a three-piece band of thirty somethings. They play surf rock, and nothing else. They cover instrumentals by Dick Dale and the Del-Tone's, the Ventures and the like. Their music epitomizes 60s surf culture and it seems to fit here. I have heard The Mexican Weirdos several times in La Paz and I'm a fan.

We leave our table to get closer to the stage. The band takes their places and twenty of us mill in front. Without fanfare they start playing Walk Don't Run by the Ventures. Next is Mr. Moto and the crowd is thrilled to hear these classics. They play hit after hit and its shocking that three musicians can produce such a diverse sound. Before taking a break, they play a precise rendition of Pipeline.

We get more beer at a Tiki bar they've opened near the dance floor. Baja Joe's is now packed, and by the time we get served the band has started playing again. The

Mexican Weirdo's launch into Out of Limits. A few songs later, they play a flawless version of Rebel Rouser followed by Misirlou. By this point everybody is dancing, and the music seems to get faster. Finally, they perform the intricate masterpiece Apache.

I will be seeing The Mexican Weirdos again in a couple of weeks. They play regularly at La Morante Art Bar. This unusual venue is my favourite club in Baja. It's a haven for artists of all types. Not only do they book the best small bands, but I have seen video installations and heard poetry readings. While you're sipping a beer in the courtyard, there might be a sculptor or painter at the back of the room.

The owner Alejandra Morante books smaller acts often overlooked elsewhere. A couple of times, I have seen a guy named El Javi. He plays a note for note rendition of Bohemian Rhapsody that moves people to tears. Perhaps my favourite nights are when Terry Townsend performs. Terry is a Grammy winning trumpet player from the US. Like many of us, he fell in love with Baja on vacation. He's made it his mission to promote Jazz in Baja and has even organized a Big Band. Sometimes he plays theme nights, his Chet Baker nights being very popular. He plays all Baker's classics and even sings "My Funny Valentine." At the back of the stage, he projects videos of Chet Baker playing horn.

After the concert, we walk to a fashionable mezcaleria a few blocks away. La Miserable imports a range of Mezcal's from small market producers near Oaxaca. Mezcal being the cousin of tequilla. Agave plants, which are its main ingredient, are burnt in pits. This gives Mezcal a distinctive smokiness and complexity. We sit at the bar and order shots while eating the lightest tamale's imaginable. Tamale's make wonderful booze mops at the end of the night. They are cornmeal filled with meat or cheese and steamed in corn husks. We sit at the bar talking about the concert and catching up with the bartenders.

The stray dog situation in towns like La Ventana is upsetting for many. Groups of scruffy strays frequently wander the streets in search of food and water. There are local initiatives to spay and neuter them. Some are even shipped to foster homes in the US and Canada.

Stray dogs are a problem throughout much of Latin America. A few years ago, I went on a hiking trip with Emily to South America. I took the Red Eye to Lima, Peru and was at the carousel getting my bag. I always pack a kilo of dog treats for the strays we will undoubtedly meet. I was passed by a cop with a sniffer dog. The dog lit up. Instantly, I was surrounded by five police with machine guns. They screamed at me to empty my bag. I undid the straps and spilled my clothes onto the floor. When they saw the Ziplock of dog treats fall, they laughed at me. I asked the cop if I could give his dog one. He scanned the room for his boss and then nodded yes.

The strays in La Ventana are friendly but skittish, particularly around men. They often run towards you, wagging their tails, but stop twenty feet away. You have to talk to them sweetly to encourage them to come within petting distance. And many are too wary to get anywhere near you. And it's for good reason. I've seen rocks thrown at them and once saw one get hit by a car. The driver didn't even stop to check the dog's broken leg. Its shrieks were unmistakable.

It's getting hot and I wake in the middle of the night and open my patio doors. I haven't put in the screens and don't think about it. Later, I hear something in the room and find my flashlight. A puppy is curled up beside my bed. He has a red collar so I know he belongs to someone. I fall back asleep. When I wake, the dog is splayed on his side in the sunshine.

He follows me downstairs, and I get him a bowl of water. He looks hungry so I search my cupboard for something to feed him. In desperation, I make a cheese omelette and put it in a bowl. The puppy smells the egg and gives a tentative lick. He then drags the omelette out of the bowl and into the sand. He makes quick work of it and smiles. I go back inside and light the stove to boil water. I post a picture of the puppy on the La Ventana Facebook group.

The puppy looks bored, and I fear he might wander away if I don't occupy him. I find a coconut for him to chew. He gnaws on it, and a couple of hours later it's in pieces. His owner finally sends a message. I let the dog put his head out the window as I drive him home a few miles away. Walking into their yard, he sees their kids and his tail wags vigorously. A handyman trims a hedge nearby.

"Did that dog destroy your house?" he asks.

"Just a coconut," I say.

"He chews more than any dog I've ever seen," he says.

I wave goodbye, and I miss the dog immediately.

Back in Time

Driving from La Paz to La Ventana takes about forty-five minutes. You cut through the more congested streets of La Paz, gradually getting to the outskirts of town. Small businesses sell car tires, cooked chickens, and beer. Several junkyards dot the highway until you are in a high desert. The road climbs rolling forested hills of deciduous trees and cactus. It rises to a pass in the mountains before dropping like a stone to the Sea of Cortez. I see an older man hitch-hiking in front of an OXXO. I pull over, and he gets in. He's friendly, but his accent is heavy, and I struggle to understand him. He's missing teeth and has an infectious smile and a hearty laugh. He points to my stereo.

"You like Grupo Niche?" he asks.

I tell him I have been listening to them for more than thirty years. I started listening to Grupo Niche on my first trip to Latin America. He says I have good taste in music, and I turn up the volume. I've always found that what we like matters. Not only is it a point of conversation, but it's a place of understanding. We come from different experiences but share a love of some of the same things.

He explains that he's going to the town of La Huerta for his best friend's birthday. As we drive, he asks me if it's that cold in Canada. I tell him that where I live, it's extremely cold and sometimes will be minus forty degrees Celsius. He shakes his head and laughs at my misery. After about twenty minutes, he points to the turn-off to La Huerta. I tell him that I can drive to his friend's house, and he smiles. I have never been here before, and I always like exploring.

La Huerta is a tiny village surrounded by rocky mountains. We pass a gate with a statue of the Virgin Mary on top. Many bouquets of plastic flowers decorate it. There is a tienda selling the essentials, but the town doesn't appear to have any other businesses. Several dogs sprawl on the road, and a cluster of thirty goats graze next to the church. All the houses have yards filled with vibrant flowering trees and bushes. He points to a dirt path that meanders away from the church and says something I don't understand. I weave between potholes until we pass through a cattle gate where the path ends.

"We're here," he says, and insists I meet his friend. We get out, and a man in a bright red shirt steps into the yard.

"Hello, my friend," says the old man. They talk a little and then I'm introduced

"I'm Mateo, and you have brought my best friend since I was a child to my birthday."

Mateo is about five-eight, with a slender build and lively eyes. He hugs the old man and then shakes my hand. Mateo invites me to have dinner with them.

"We're having Arrachera," he says. This flank steak is often marinated for hours, and BBQ'd over mesquite.

I explain that I have to meet friends and can't stay long. Mateo doesn't seem convinced and leads me into his house. He pushes a massive wooden door, and we step into the entry. Sunlight streams into the back of the house, and the living room is bathed in feathery brightness. The room is simple and lived-in. Everything ancient with rustic, rough-hewn tables and chairs. Silvery barn wood decorates a back wall. It's evident Mateo has exceptional taste. He watches my attention and tells me stories about anything that catches my eye. There is too much to see and too many stories to hear, and after ten minutes, we step onto the deck. It hangs over the deep arroyo. Mateo explains that people have been living here for hundreds if not thousands of years. As a result, the arroyo is now full of fruit trees growing wild. He points to a large bowl full of papaya, mango, banana, and a few fruits I've never even heard of before that he's collected.

"It's my grocery store," he says, pointing into the valley. "This Arroyo has the sweetest water. Everything grows here."

He pulls a piece of terracotta from a nearby pail. It's a pottery shard with an intricate zigzag pattern on it.

"I found this over there," he says, pointing to the yard.

"That looks old," I say, picking up the pottery from his hand.

"It could be thousands of years old; who knows?" He says. "People came for the water. They knew."

Mateo lifts a couple of stone micro blades from a table and passes them to me.

"They used these to cut meat," he says.

"This one looks like a spear point," I say.

"They hunted too," he says.

I'm astonished by the wealth of treasures he keeps on his deck. He walks over to a giant white bucket under a tree in his garden. He bends over and lifts out a two-foot fossilized shell that looks like a unicorn horn.

"There are lots of fossils here too," he says matter-of-factly.

"That could be a million years old," I say.

"This mountain used to be on the bottom of the ocean," he explains.

He lifts out fossils of tropical plants and a variety of sea-shells embedded in rock. We empty the bucket like palae-ontologists. Everything at Mateo's house is old, and he lives amongst these artifacts. His collection rivals many museums I have visited. After a couple of hours, I explain that I'm late to meet my friends at the horse race in Los Planes. Soon his other guests will be arriving, and the mesquite will be lit. I wish him a happy birthday and promise to visit again soon.

I drive down the long road towards the sea a little quicker than normal. I'm late to meet my friends at the horse races. I don't know where they are being held but

Los Planes isn't so big. I pass the La Ventana turn-off and am soon in Los Planes. I see cars and trucks turning onto a dirt road to the right. I follow them blindly through the desert, before coming to a large field. There's two long rows of vehicles and between them is the race track. I park between a couple of pick-ups. A woman comes up to me and sells me a ticket for a couple of dollars. The ticket entitles me to a beer, she says.

There are several hundred people milling around on both sides of the track. It feels like a country fair, and I feel at home. The girls travel in groups of four or five and wear fancy dresses with ribbons in their hair. The boys are in their best jeans and cowboy hats. Families sit in the back of pickup trucks, eating delicious smelling foods. When I meet my friends, they tell me that the horse races are about to start. The track is still being prepped. At the start line a pick-up truck pulls a large steel bar to smooth the sand. We lean over the fence as two horses enter the gate. With the pop of a starter's pistol the gate is thrown open. The horses explode and charge down the track. The crowd screams. They're neck and neck for most of the race. Then one horse pulls ahead by a couple feet at the end. People hug and cheer. That's the first race of nine.

I go to a pick-up with many flats of beer stacked at the back. Cans are buried in ice in a few coolers. I give my ticket and am handed an ice cold Tecate beer. I return to my friends and wait for the next race to begin.

After five or six races, it starts to feel a little monotonous. The locals, however, are having a wonderful time. People get their pictures taken with the winning horses and riders. There isn't anywhere I would rather be.

The following morning when I wake, I feel restless. From my deck I drink my coffee and study the vast landscape. For a couple years, I've been practicing meditation and even belong to a group that meets weekly. Once a season we go for a weeklong retreat at a resort called Casa Tara.

Casa Tara is an impressive place with a large meeting room with an intricate palapa roof. It has a labyrinth that visitors can use. I often try to arrive early so I could walk it. The labyrinth is a spiral with rock borders. And their kitchen serves healthy food that is well-prepared. Once the chef apologized that desert was sweetened with honey and wasn't vegan. Did he grind up bees in this thing? I thought.

Sipping my coffee, it occurs to me that I have room in front of my house for a labyrinth of my own. The family that cleared the brush left an expanse of more than fifty feet of empty sand. I know that there's a beach beyond Hot Springs Beach that has many fist-sized rocks. I put a couple of five-gallon pails into the van and grab my coffee. I drive past Hot Springs Beach and up a hill before coming to a rocky beach. I park as close to the surf as I can get. Around the van are perfectly sized stones and I fill my pails.

At the house, I struggle with the weight of the buckets. I place them in front of the house and then consider my options. I grab my rake, which is rest against the side of the house. Its width is perfect, I think. I drop a rock for a center and then drag the rake in a spiral pattern around it. It is a foot wide and gives me eight rings. I make a scuff mark every couple of feet where I will place the rocks. I then drop a rock on the scuff marks. After, I start to fill in between these rocks. Before long, I'm going back to the beach for more rocks. By noon, I have a spiralling labyrinth. I walked it slowly in the mid-day heat.

I'm not just battling scorpions, but mice have been giving me problems, as well. If I go away for even a few days, a family of mice will move in. They'll chew up my things and leave shit everywhere. I've spent hours cleaning and sanitizing. I just don't feel people and mice can coexist. It's like saying "kind of pregnant." There is no middle ground with mice. You either have them or you don't.

I tried a couple of live traps I bought in Mexico. They had a spring-loaded door and I never caught a single mouse. In desperation, I bought some traditional kill traps but I hated using them. So, I brought a couple of traps down from Canada. They are aluminum boxes with a big clear window along the top. Inescapable doors are at either end. A mouse will smell the bait and go in the trap. Once it realizes it's trapped, it will scream. Other mice will come and they'll end up in the trap too. Sometimes, I'll have four or five mice in the trap in the morning. I drive them to a remote beach and let them go.

It feels as though I'm constantly beating back pests. I sweep dung beetles out of my house every morning. Sometimes, I see five or six ants and later there are a million. You have to be vigilant and willing to get your hands dirty.

PUDDLE OF PEE

I go to my favorite sushi restaurant for lunch, Odayaka Sushi Bar at Marina Costa Baja. As I take a seat, the owner's daughter, comes over. She's from Tijuana and is always fun.

"Are you going to Carnival?" I ask.

"Not anymore," she says.

"Why not?"

"Because every time I go to Carnival, I end up standing in a puddle of pee," she says, rolling her eyes. I'm intrigued, but she leaves to take a drink order of a couple taking a table on the other side of the porch. I order a couple of rolls and a beer from a passing waiter. I savor them looking at the expensive yachts in the harbor.

Carnival is the best. An enormous street festival that goes on for five days. Some years, I'll go every single night. There's always good music, exciting food, rides, and a lot more to see and do. On this night, I go to carnival with Brian and Michelle. We start the evening with dinner at El Mesquite. Celia meets us at the entrance. She gives me a hug and shows us to a table in the corner. We order margaritas. The bartender squeezes Colima limes into glasses. Soon we're sipping the most delicious margaritas imaginable. I order the tuna, and they have hamburgers.

This restaurant makes everything fresh to order. A heavy-set grill man stands attentively behind a mesquite fire at the front of the restaurant. I can see him searing the tuna, turning it after only a few minutes. Another cook plates salad and then drizzles a marinade over the tuna from a squeeze bottle. It's simple and fresh—one of the best meals in the Baja.

Celia brings us the plates, and we order more margaritas. The tuna has deep grill marks. When I cut into it, the meat is bright red and lukewarm. In a word: perfect. The tuna dissolves on my tongue. I have to remember to breathe. El Mesquite always gets it right.

I leave the van in front of the restaurant. We walk a couple of blocks downhill to the Malecon. The din of Carnival makes talking difficult, and we're not even there yet.

Carnival stretches more than twenty blocks, and the street is already crowded. Bandstands dot our route. We weave through the crowd to Norteno musicians and various young bands playing Latin classics. Many seem to perform Selena covers, the songstress who was murdered by her manager twenty years earlier.

We stop and get a bag of Churros, a type of Mexican donut. I opt for cinnamon sugar rather than Cajeta, a caramel sauce. The sweet and fat are an irresistible combination as we weave through the crowd. Kiosks sell novelties, including the ubiquitous Luchadora masks. I suppose there's nothing better than going to a fair dressed as a Mexican wrestler. Girls buy plastic tiaras. I see a grandmother wearing a thick mustache to her laughing family. While it feels crowded, you know that it will be much worse later.

There is a kid's area with small rides. Fathers stand next to children riding horses on merry-go-rounds. A tiny Ferris wheel is rotating in the night. We backtrack to the central area of the Malecon. Stands sell cakes, pizza, and corndogs. Enormous bars hawk 16-ounce plastic cups of cocktails like Cuba Libre's and Pina Coladas. Some sell a Micheladas, beer, Clamato, lime, and God-knows-what-else concoction popular in Mexico.

We stand behind a barricade as the parade starts. Flat-bed semis filled with people dancing and dressed as Hawaiians or Romans slowly pass us. Several marching bands step in unison and groups of dancers keep the beat. Floats with dragons, dolphins and other animals drift down the Malecon. It's informal and charming. The crowd claps and waves at the spectacle.

After the parade, Michelle leads us towards the rides. She intends to go on everything scary. Brian says that he's not interested in going on any rides. I go to the ticket counter and buy a few tickets. I join Michelle in a line. Back home, we would call it the "Zipper." We're locked standing beside each other in a cage. I study the welds of the ride's mechanism. I don't know anything about welding and scrutinize the beaded metal, looking for cracks. After about a dozen cages are filled, the ride starts. We climb a hundred feet and drop facing the ground. Michelle is screaming and laughing. I close my eyes in terror. The ride speeds up, and we weightlessly hurdle to the ground. When it stops, the cage is opened, and I stagger back into the crowd.

"Let's go on that one," says Michelle, pointing.

"It's called the Nauseator," I say.

Undeterred, she gets in another line.

I knew this ride as "The Hurricane" as a kid. It looks like I might have been on this actual ride even. All the rides look like antiques from long-forgotten fairs back home. Some even have labels from American carnivals. This ride is a big circle where you are strapped against the wall. It spins and tilts on its side. It's not as bad as the Zipper, but I start to taste the Churros. Michelle takes the next ride alone.

By this point, the Malecon is swollen with an unimaginably dense crowd. Since it's getting late, we head to the main bandstand. Claudia at Casa Parra had told me that Grupo Canaveral is performing. I'm a big fan of theirs and seeing them live is a fantastic opportunity. Knowing that we could be stuck in a crowd for a while, we stop for a beer. We push through the crowd for the next half hour before reaching the main stage.

A five-piece is playing a medley of Salsa hits when we arrive. Their lead singer is wearing a full-length diva dress. The lights behind her flash bright patterns and colors. The crowd is positioning themselves for the main act. Grupo Canaveral is the most popular Cumbia band in Mexico. They are from Mexico City and have numerous hits. One of their singers is the octogenarian Humberto Pabon. His unmistakable squeals are beloved throughout Latin America.

To see Grupo Canaveral, we're going to need to be closer to the stage. We start moving through the audience. Spaces open, allowing us to step forward. In fifteen minutes of shuffling, we're in the middle of the audience.

But the crowd is growing.

"We have to go," says Brian, leaning to my ear. "This is too crowded for us."

I nod my head instead of trying to talk above the din.

Finally, the warm-up act plays their last song. Roadies break down the stage to prepare for Grupo Canaveral. Brian and Michelle point to an area at the back they hope to stand at. I continue to move forward, and soon I can touch the stage. I look at my phone for several minutes. Other friends are posting pictures from different places in Carnaval on Facebook. Familiar kiosks and ride photographs and everybody is having fun.

The crowd starts to clap and shout as the MC introduces Grupo Canaveral. Ten thousand scream as the band walks onto the stage. Humberto Pabon is last and is led by the elbow to a stool. The crowd goes nuts when they see him. The band launches into Flores En Febrero, one of their biggest hits. The screen behind them strobes wildly. Three glitter cannons blast tinsel into the air. Five dancers dressed in Danskins and knee boots dance in unison across the stage. It's time to strap in for an unforgettable performance. The audience sings with every lyric and inflection. It's a sea of people—the wall of sound harmonious, joyous, and alive. The chaos continues for the next hour and a half without a break. The front row is covered in glitter. It's the best party

I've ever been to. I will be finding glitter when I shower for months after.

The crowd mills and thins, and after fifteen minutes, I find Brian and Michelle at the back. We walk to a bar, and I get a 16-ounce sloppy Margarita. Made with lime mix and the cheapest tequila they can find, it's a far cry from the ones from dinner. But it hits the spot and takes the edge off my adrenaline from the concert. We wander until about two. The crowd shrinks, but it's apparent things will be going until sunrise. We stand sipping our drinks, listening to a man hawk blankets. He speaks fast into a headset microphone and the volume is deafening. Who comes to Carnival to buy a blanket? I wonder. Then I watch several people line-up to get one. I look down and see that an outhouse nearby has overflowed. I'm standing in a large puddle of pee. Carnival is over for another year.

Work continues at the house as we approach the Easter holidays. Semana Santa is in a couple of days. It's the calm before the storm. Already, locals are staking their tents and positioning barbecues on the beach. I get a call from a friend in Los Barriles. Erin is a retired operating room nurse and kiteboarding instructor. She invites me to Passover Seder, knowing that I'm of Jewish heritage.

I wasn't raised in the Jewish faith but definitely in the Jewish culture. My grandmother, an Orthodox Jew, escaped the Nazis in France. She climbed through the Pyrenees with my mother and aunt with the Nazis on their heels. When they got to Spain, they were put in a refugee camp for a year before immigrating to Canada. My grandmother was a badass. She was also one of the lucky ones. Of her seven siblings, only two escaped Auschwitz.

My mother raised me Catholic. It always felt strange to be going to church with a mother who spoke Yiddish.

"Put down your bagels; we're late for church," she would yell on Sunday mornings. Later I came to understand the war had left her traumatized. She never wanted her children singled out the way she had been. So, she hid us in Catholicism. For six years, I spent my Sundays confused studying Catechism. When I was thirteen and a week away from Confirmation, I told her I didn't believe in Jesus. She screwed up her face and kicked me in the shin - and she was wearing clogs. She then took my brother and sisters out for ice cream sundaes. Rubbing my leg, I told my father about the confrontation.

"Leave me out of it," he said and went back to reading the weekend sports section.

I thought that going to Seder would be a good opportunity to explore my Jewish roots. She said a rabbi in Cabo had even donated Matzo. I drove the twisty mountain road 50 kilometres to reach her place. Los Bareilles is a neighbouring kiteboarding and fishing community. It's older, bigger, and more established than La Ventana. In La Ventana, people say, "please don't let this town end up like Los Bareilles."

I had never been to Erin's, and she gave a full tour. Her house is modern with lots of local arts and crafts. The living room leads to a spacious porch. I'm impressed with the mature fruit trees in her yard. The beach is two blocks away, and she's only a stone's throw to the strip.

We walk to the house hosting the Seder. It belongs to an American couple, and one of them is an architect, though I can't remember which one. The house has an expansive deck with a palapa roof—an enormous dining table stretched along one side. Dinner starts after an hour of mingling. Everyone I meet is curious about why anyone would build a house in La Ventana.

The fifteen guests take their places at the table. After a brief greeting, we have a toast of a crisp white wine. A paper with the Seder story is passed from person to person. Each of us read a paragraph or two. It tells the story of the Jews gaining their freedom from slavery from the Egyptians. Most of us have limited knowledge of the tradition. However, there is a Jewish yoga instructor who fills in the gaps. After the story comes an array of Jewish delicacies, including the Matzo the rabbi had given. Many of the foods represent the bitterness of slavery and various aspects of the slavery experience.

We end up reclining on couches in the living room, talking. Erin and I walk back to her house, and she tells me about her ex-husband, who was Jewish. She invites me to stay in her guest room, but I felt a burning need to get back to La Paz. Emily will be arriving in a day, and there were many things I need to prepare. I gave Erin a hug and pull out of her driveway shortly before midnight.

The first twenty minutes go well. There isn't much traffic on the mountain road. I fear drunk drivers as I heard scary stories about Semana Santa drunks. As I approach El Triunfo, however, I can barely keep my eyes open and fear I will drive off a cliff. I pull into a gravel pit and unfold my bed. Within seconds, I'm sound asleep.

I wake a few hours later. I get out of the van and have a pee. The warm night air is comforting and still. It's after four, and I can be in La Paz in time for an early breakfast. I climb into the driver's seat and pull onto the highway. I notice immediately I'm having difficulty seeing the road. The median is faded and dim. I drive slowly, making sure I don't go off any cliffs. At the edge of town, I approach a police checkpoint. A bored cop waves me through without looking up from his phone.

The streetlights of La Paz help me see better, but it's still tricky making things out. As I get downtown, I see that they've closed the Malecon for the festivities. I turn onto a street running parallel and make my way through town. A cop on a street corner waves for me to stop. It's almost 6 a.m., and a tired-looking cop walks up to the van.

"Good morning," he says.

"Hi," I reply.

"Have you been drinking?"

"I had a couple of glasses of wine with dinner last night. But I'm not drunk or anything," I say.

"The reason I ask is that you're swerving," he says.

"I'm having difficulty seeing the road," I reply.

"That's because you don't have your headlights on," he says.

I realize I drove through the mountains from El Triunfo without headlights. I burst out laughing.

"I can't believe I did that," I say.

The cop looks at me as if I'm insane.

"Okay, try not to kill anyone," he says and waves me through. I turn on my headlights, drive a few blocks, and get a cup of coffee.

I spend the day in La Paz running errands and taking care of tasks I've ignored for months. The following morning, I wake early and drive to San Jose del Cabo International Airport. I park an hour before Emily's flight. I always have trouble estimating how much time the drive to the airport takes. I walk to a nearby OXXO and get a bottle of Topo Chico. This is the Evian or Perrier of Mexico and, to my taste, equal. That means it's just another fizzy water, but it hits the spot. I'm not a connoisseur of water.

I lean against a wall at Arrivals—a swarm of taxi drivers and tour operators jockey outside. When Emily walks into the lounge, I throw my arms around her. She looks great. Her cheeks rosy and her curly hair wild from months of riding a mountain bike through Patagonia. I carry her bag to the van, and we drive to Cerritos on the peninsula's west side.

Cerritos is one of the most impressive beaches anywhere. Miles of pristine sand curls towards a rocky headland. On the north end of the beach is one of the best right-hand breaks in Baja. Above this impressive wave is a colonial-style hotel. It's painted a rich orange, and its dome looms. I change into a swim shirt and grab my boogie board. Emily climbs into the back, gets her bathing suit from her bag, and changes. We rent her a board from a kiosk on the beach.

Boogie boards are made of lightweight foam and only a few feet long.

"I love this!" she says, walking into the water. Forty-five minutes earlier, she was at the airport, and now she's in the Pacific.

We push ourselves through the chilly surf until we're chest deep. We turn to face the beach and launch ourselves onto the next wave and take off. The wave steepens, and we collide and laugh before getting tossed and rinsed in the foam. My board shorts have pulled down and I jostle to tighten the drawstring. We push ourselves back through the surf to catch many more.

After a couple of hours, we stagger onto the beach. We return the boogie board and walk to the van. I lean my head onto my shoulder and hop to unplug my ears. We drive to Baja Beans, a nearby coffee shop. We sit outside under a tree. The table is an old wooden door; its weathered and stunning. Emily sips her black pour-over with her eyes squinting in the warmth.

"This is one of the best coffees I've ever had," she says. This is quite a compliment. Emily is a discriminating coffee drinker.

"They roast on-site," I say.

We savor our coffee while she gives me the highlights of her adventure in South America. When we get back to the van, our hair is nearly dry.

"Are you hungry?" I ask while I back out of the parking space.

"I'm always hungry now."

"I know a place that makes the best pizza in the Baja,"
I say.

"A pizza would be perfect."

We turn onto the highway and head north on the four-
lane road. A little way later, it divides, and we head away
from Todos Santos and the setting sun. Soon, we're in the
mountains and parked in front of El Triunfo Cafe.

We take a seat in the brick-lined courtyard and order a
large salad and a pizza margarita. When the pizza arrives, we
have drunk half our tall lemonades, and our stomachs growl.
The pizza looks enormous, and I worry that we won't be
able to eat half of it. But this isn't much of an issue. When
we're done, all that remains are crumbs, and the salad bowl
is reduced to a tiny smear of olive oil. Emily has a blissed-
out look, and we start the short journey down the hill to La
Ventana.

I'm eager to show Emily all the reasons I moved to Baja.
I alternate days where we drive with days spent at the beach
in La Ventana. Emily appreciates the simplicity of snorkelling
a reef all afternoon. She meets Chava, Carlos, and the others.
Chava seems surprised she's a physicist and asks her lots of
questions. We eat at all the local restaurants. Many afternoons
we have Mango Margaritas at Palapas Ventana. I want to
share my enthusiasm for Baja but not oversell.

Each day, I have a rough itinerary of things I would
like to show her. One morning, we drive up the peninsula past the port of Pichelingue to Balandra. This beach is

often ranked in the top ten of the most beautiful beaches in the world. It's a shallow, sandy bay, which you can walk across. Rocky cliffs surround the beach. Families pitch beach umbrellas and empty the most oversized coolers you have ever seen. Wandering vendors sell cold beer and cups of fruit. Emily and I walk the knee-deep water to the famous mushroom rock. This pile of conglomerate rock sits at the exit of the bay. There's already a lineup of locals taking pictures next to it.

We drive the two kilometres north to Tecolote Beach. It faces Isla Espiritu Santos. A rocky, uninhabited island that is part of a large marine park. We walk to an open-air bar to get a drink. A fellow Canadian named Gary is already sitting at the bar. I have never been to this bar without him being there. He never wears a shirt, opting for an open leather vest and cowboy hat. When he sees me, he gives me a friendly fist bump. I introduce Emily, and we order a limonada and sit at a table in the sand.

It's Semana Santa, and campers and tents line the beach half a dozen deep. This beach is huge but now feels crowded. Families in lawn chairs surround barbecues and coolers shaded by awnings and tarps. Multi-generations share the simple pleasures of being together. Their enthusiasm is infectious. When we finish our drinks, we go for a swim and watch long-nosed needlefish dart around us. Dripping wet, we buy a cup of sliced mango. The vendor insists on sprinkling Tajin. Mexicans prefer to have chilly spice on their fruit. But we opt for a squeeze of lime instead. It's the first mango I've had this season, and it's sweet and delicious.

We walk to a nearby restaurant and luckily find an open table at the back. We'd prefer to sit closer to the water. But that would need a long wait, and we're too hungry for that. Three musicians approach us and ask if we have a request. I panic trying to remember Latin songs and blurt out "Besame Mucho" (Kiss me a Lot). Emily is humiliated that I've chosen the piece ninety percent of all Gringo's request.

"It's all I could think of," I try to explain.

The singer exaggerates every note, and I can sense Emily's discomfort. It strikes me as funny, and I smile at the band. When they're done, I give them a couple of bucks. They tilt their hats and leave.

"Well, that was embarrassing," says Emily.

"That's what fathers are for," I tell her.

I used to come to this restaurant every Sunday. It's an excellent place to get rustic-style seafood. The fishermen land their boats only a few hundred feet down the beach. When you order a snapper, the waiter asks how hungry you are. He then walks next door to buy a suitably sized fish. After a couple of weeks of showing up with a dozen friends, overwhelming the kitchen with orders, the waiter asks if we would like to eat "Mexican style."

"What's that?" I ask.

"Instead of individual orders, we'll just bring out food," he explains. I must have hesitated too long because he disappears into the back, returning with an enormous grouper still dripping wet from the sea.

"We could cook this," he says. We look at the behemoth and say a quick "hell yeah!"

A half-hour later, he lumbers under an enormous platter of fried fish. Another waiter ferries piles of tortillas, rice, beans, guacamole, and salsa. It's a ridiculous tower of food. As the sun sets, we devour every morsel on that table. After this feast, we return weekly to eat "Mexican Style."

POWER TO THE PEOPLE

In the old section of La Paz is a fashionable restaurant named Nim. I try to get there whenever I can. Ducking out for an afternoon cocktail is one of my favorite things. Nim makes terrific drinks. I especially like their mojitos. They use sparkling water instead of 7-Up. It makes the drink less sweet and the mint more striking. My friend Jack is with me. He's from Kansas and likes super sweet cocktails and fast food. He talks about the mudslides he orders at TGI Fridays with reverence. I once told him about a drink called a "Redneck Margarita" as a joke. It's tequila mixed with Mountain Dew. A few days later, he had one waiting for me when I visited. He said he wished I had told him about them sooner. Embarrassed, I gulped my Redneck Margarita, trying not to wince.

The artwork in the restaurant is a series by Ulysses Martinez. They are lithographs of various Baja animals and birds, and most are monochrome. I wander around the restaurant viewing the collection. One print of a Roadrunner is especially compelling. It's a close-up of the Roadrunners head, and it's staring straight at you as if to say, "What the fuck are you looking at?" There is a stylized Cardon and another desert plant that is familiar, but I don't know its name in the background. I sit down at my table but get up three times to see the print before finishing my mojito.

The print is enormous: Four feet wide and three feet tall. I have always felt that a house doesn't need lots of art. But the art needs to be strong. I knew it would look great between the two dark bathroom doors in my kitchen. The Roadrunner would be the first thing you saw when you walked in the door.

I had met the owner of the restaurant a few times. She's intelligent and always made interesting conversations. She speaks fluent English and likes to talk about local art. I notice her sitting at a table across the room doing book-keeping. I head to her table and ask about the print. She explains Ulysses Martinez came from the mainland but now lives in La Paz. He had done a lot of street art and was now exploring printmaking. And the Roadrunner print is also her favorite.

"Is it for sale?" I ask.

"It's $400. Framed," she says.

I had been to the bank and have a pocketful of cash.

"I'll take it," I tell her.

She smiles and asks my waiter to take the print off the wall. She then wraps it in brown paper for the ride home.

I go back to the table and tell Jack that I bought the print. He doesn't seem surprised or interested. A person who drinks a Redneck Margarita is not an arbiter of taste. After paying for the print and drinks, I slide it into the back of the van.

When I get home, I place the Roadrunner against the kitchen wall. I stand across the room to admire the print and feel a gratitude for finding such a brilliant piece. I get out my drill and soon have a hanger mounted. I lift the print onto the hook. It makes the room come alive. I invite a few friends to see it. I open a bottle of Cabernet. I sip the wine while examing the print from every angle possible.

In the morning, I visit Jeff in North Arroyo. He's a revered kiteboarder in his sixties. He's well-read and self-taught in most things. I knock on his door, and he invites me into the camper. He's still lying in bed and reading a Louis L'Amour novel.

"I forgot I invited you," he says.

"Do you want me to turn on the kettle?" I ask.

"Please," he says.

I put the kettle in the sink and fill it—his water pump thrumming.

"Yeah, I need to fix that," he says

I put the kettle on the stovetop and light the propane. I wince with the pungency of the match's sulfur. We can hear a couple of men arguing about the best way to tow their truck off the beach.

Jeff gets a text from his daughter. He tells me his daughter is late on her rent and needs another loan. He says loan with quotation marks. He sits up in bed and grabs his iPad. I can see an ad for a kite on his screen. A week earlier, he said he was looking for a new twelve metre kite. He looks at it for a few seconds and then opens his banking app and transfers the money. He types a note with the transfer.

"How's this sound?" he asks. "You should consider making up with your mom. After all, she's a doctor. Love you always, Dad."

"Sounds good," I tell him. "It points her in the right direction for getting money in the future."

"That's the hope," he says. "I don't want to get in another fight with her."

He climbs out of bed naked and pulls on his faded board shorts. He puts on a worn t-shirt with "Duracell" written across the front.

"I'll be a second," and he steps into the blazing Mexican sunshine. He walks up a short hill to the restroom. He stands in line with two other kiters. They are in their 20s, have dreadlocks and many tattoos. They talk and soon are laughing.

Five minutes later, he's back in the camper. We can still hear the men debating how to pull the truck out of the sand. Jeff puts some coffee into a stainless-steel French press and fills it with boiling water. There's a knock at the door. The two guys arguing are asking for his help.

"I'll be out as soon as my coffee is ready," he tells them.

A few minutes later, we're walking down the beach with our coffees. The truck is up to its axles in the soft sand.

"You are stucked," says Jeff, trying to make it sound like "fucked."

Jeff takes a long nylon tow strap from his backpack and attaches a metal hook to the truck's frame. He then walks to some Mexican fishermen launching a panga farther down the beach. A few minutes later, a rusty old Toyota truck backs up. Jeff attaches the tow strap to the ball on their trailer hitch. He asks them to pull forward slowly. The tow strap goes taut. Jeff walks over to the cab of the stranded truck and tells the driver to creep out of the hole slowly. Jeff stresses the word "slowly." The driver starts his engine, and Jeff stands to the side, guiding him with his hands.

"Va!" he yells to the Mexican driver. Its wheels spin before gaining traction. The stuck truck lurches out of the sand and is back on the hard pack. Jeff signals to them to stop. He detaches the strap from the Toyota's trailer hitch. He walks back to the truck and tells him to give the Mexican driver a couple of hundred pesos for the effort.

We go back to Jeff's trailer and finish our coffees. His iPad hums, and he checks it.

"Thanks, Dad. You're a lifesaver," Jeff reads aloud. "I'm saving lots of people today."

After leaving Jeff's, I go swimming at Hot Springs Beach. On my way home, I notice a sign zip-tied to a fence. It's for a solar systems company. I text them asking for information. When I get home, the owner of the company has replied. He asks about my house and where I'm located. His office is in La Paz, but he has a place in El Sargento. I tell him I want solar panels, batteries, a controller, a refrigerator, and a water heater. He has a package price that includes almost everything I need plus installation. It's roughly what I expected to pay. He says he's going to El Sargento the next day and will visit.

Electricity in Baja Sur is generated at a plant near La Paz. This plant supplies power to Cabo, Todos Santos, and many small towns and communities throughout southern Baja. It burns diesel. Five tall smokestacks purge yellow sulfurous exhaust day and night. Tanker ships land three or four times a week five miles north of town. When I bought my place, I vowed to be off grid.

The next afternoon, Tomas visits. He's a friendly fifty-year-old and climbs the ladder to the rooftop. He says there's lots of room for everything.

"It will be a quick and easy install," he says.

We climb down to the yard, and he says he can start work the next day. He has everything in his shop, and his crew is available.

"Terrific," I say.

Tomas attaches a credit card reader to his phone. I make a thousand-dollar deposit.

At ten the following day, his crew of five arrives. Four

men and a young woman. They are in their twenties except for a foreman in his fifties. Jose has a weathered face and always wears foam knee pads. He complains of a sore stomach frequently.

They climb to the roof and start making plans. Soon, they are unloading solar panels from their truck. They pass the panels to the rooftop from the upstairs landing. They run wires to the bodega where I want them to install the controller, batteries, and other equipment. I want to muffle sound and have a convenient location so I can easily monitor the system.

For the next week, the crew drills holes and stays busy. They mount stout aluminum frames to keep the panels from flying away in a hurricane. The far wall of the bodega soon has two electrical panels, a solar controller, and an inverter to change DC power to AC.

Tomas calls and says that my solar refrigerator has arrived. It operates on 12v power, is very efficient, and is built for solar systems like mine. I chose a chest refrigerator without a freezer because it's even more efficient.

I jump in the van and drive to pick it up in La Paz. I find Tomas's office at a closed restaurant he owns using Google Maps. We unwrap and unbox the refrigerator and slide it into the van. Fortunately, it's light and small. It has a strange locking mechanism to prevent your kids from sneaking treats.

At home, I place the refrigerator beside the counter. Jose plugs it in. I now have a couple of working electrical outlets in the kitchen. It hums to life, and soon I feel a slight chill on the interior wall. I drive to Star Market and pick up an eight-pack of beer to celebrate. I buy light beer because the men are at work and need to drive back to La Paz at the end of the day. I also picked up a carton of Half and Half cream, thrilled that I can make coffee in the morning. When I return, the crew puts away their tools for the day. I hand everyone a beer.

"You know, when you offer us light beer, it's like you're calling us gay," Jose says.

I'm surprised that Jose says this. I also regret that my Spanish isn't better. I wish I could say, "I'm just worried about your figure, sweetheart."

It dawns on me that the crew might think I'm gay. I'm a single guy living in a pink house, after all. In fairness, many people back home would have thought the same thing under similar circumstances. I prepare dinner while they drive away.

Later, I notice the refrigerator doesn't turn off. The compressor runs until everything starts to freeze. I empty its contents and unplug it for an hour with the top open. I turn the thermostat to its lowest setting and put my food back inside. I'm confident that the problem is fixed, and I had used the wrong setting.

The following morning, I head downstairs eager to have coffee with real cream. I boil the water, and when I open the fridge, it's frozen solid.

"Fuck!"

When the crew arrives, I explain to Jose that the thermostat is broken. He puts his hand inside the unit.

"No, it's fine," he says.

I check the fridge throughout the day, and it's always running. I tell Jose that it won't stop cycling, but he doesn't believe me.

"It's good," he repeats.

In the late afternoon, I take evasive action.

"Jose, I would like to get beer for you," I say. "What's your favorite kind?"

"I love Tecate Red," he says. "Not Blue, Red."

Tecate Blue is the gay, light kind, and he made sure I was buying heterosexual beer.

After they leave, I put an 8-pack of Tecate Red in the fridge. The next day is Friday.

Late in the afternoon, when it's sweltering, I offer the crew a beer.

"I have Tecate Red," I say. "It's Jose's favorite."

"Thank you," Jose says, taking the beer I pass him. He jiggles the can and realizes it's frozen solid. He puts his hand inside the fridge and touches the wall.

"This is impossible," he says, twisting the dial of the thermostat.

He gets a screwdriver from his tool belt and removes the vent from the side. He isn't an appliance repairman and looks at the inner workings the way I look at a car's engine. He picks up his phone and steps outside for a few minutes.

"Tomas will check the refrigerator next week," he says and then goes to the bodega to finish some wiring. I have finally got Jose's attention.

A couple of days later, the refrigerator isn't working at all. It's dead. I send Tomas a few texts, and two days later, he visits. He's an electrical engineer and says it isn't fixable after poking around for an hour.

"I'll get another shipped from Tijuana where they're made," he says. "It will take a week."

Tomas explains that I have a bigger electrical problem. When they build homes like mine, they install flexible plastic hoses in the walls. They slide the electrical wires through the hose to reach outlets and lights. It's thin-walled and sometimes gets pinched by blocks and mortar. While I had outlets and places in the ceiling for lights, the crew couldn't get the wires to them because the hose is collapsed. But he knew a mason who could cut a channel in the walls. His crew will then be able to run the wires. He pulls out his card reader, and I make another payment.

The next day, a muscular teenager from El Sargento arrives on a dirt bike. He sees my three-pound sledgehammer and starts chiseling a two-inch-wide channel in the wall. It's slow going, and for more than a week, he chips a maze of channels on the exterior of the house. I hate the constant pounding and seeing freshly painted walls get reduced to dust.

Once enough channels in the walls are exposed, the crew returns. They run new electrical wires and connect outlets, switches, and lights. In the end, each floor has a few electrical outlets. A dozen LED fixtures are mounted in the ceiling throughout the house. I'm no longer living in the nineteenth century and have power.

It has been weeks, and I haven't received the replacement fridge yet. Tomas is now putting me off and rarely replying to my texts. The mason fills all the electrical channels with mortar. Then he stuccoes and paints and the house starts to look good again. He is a good mason but a sloppy painter. I complain about splatters, and he spends a day with steel wool cleaning the concrete floors.

Getting to this point has taken far too much effort. I still don't have hot water or a refrigerator, and I'm impatient. To speed things up, I assemble the solar water heater and, using a rope, lift it onto the roof. When the crew arrives, I show Jose the instructions to the unit and where I think things should go. Jose has different ideas and says the instructions are wrong. I reason that he's the pro and leave him to do his work.

For the next couple of weeks, Jose comes a couple of days each week and fumbles around on the roof. During this time, the replacement refrigerator arrives, taking a month, not the estimated week. But like the first one, it's starts to struggle. The temperature in the unit swings wildly. In the end, it's determined that they didn't install enough battery capacity. They add two more batteries in the bodega, and it starts working correctly.

My friend Michael is staying with me while his boat is painted. Michael worked as a journalist but became a house contractor in Oregon. He has a practical problem-solving approach and is knowledgeable about a shocking number of things.

We spend a couple of mornings on the roof trying to understand what Jose is doing. Much of it doesn't make any sense to us. We go to La Paz to see another friend's solar water heater. He has the same unit, and his system works well. Michael sketches a diagram of what the working system should look like.

"Today is the two-month anniversary of my first payment to your company," I text Tomas. "I need you to come Monday and finish the job."

I attach a photo of Michael's diagram. A minute later, I get a reply of two thumbs-up emojis. Within an hour, the mason from El Sargento shows up on his motorcycle. He starts chipping a channel for a hot water pipe down my back wall. Finally, we have a workable plan. Clearly, my Assertiveness Training at the School of Chava is paying-off.

On Monday morning, I head to the roof with Tomas and Jose. The water tanks are moved where I originally wanted them. They removed a pump they had installed that served no purpose. A hot water line is connected to the upstairs shower. A switch for a pump in the water tank is wired into the bedroom. By Wednesday, I have hot water and they're done.

FORGIVENESS?

When I bought the house, there was a water tank in the back yard to irrigate the nine coconut palms. Around the tank was a five-foot wall. I smash the top two rows of cinder block with a sledgehammer. Soon, the five-foot square has walls that are only a few feet high, which is perfect for a raised bed garden. I lay the broken bits of brick on the bottom and cover them with many buckets of sand. The mason returns and stuccos the walls of the planter. He works as the sky darkens and a storm forms to the south.

An opaque wall of rain obscures the view of the mountains. I busy myself by taking all the cushions off the deck and ensuring all the windows are closed and the house is secure. I walk around my yard and make sure there aren't any tools left out. A drizzle soon leads to a heavy downpour. The leaves bounce in the pounding rain. The wind whistles against the ladder with a shrieking scream. After a punishing hour, the wind and the rain soften, and the sun comes out. The house hasn't leaked a drop. Not a single puddle anywhere.

A couple of days later, I paint the planter a bright white to match the back of the house. I call a local

landscaping supplier for a 50/50 mixture of sand and com-
post, and it's delivered the following day. Kevin, the knowledgeable owner, looks at my planter.

"If you can't grow in this soil in that planter, you're in
trouble" he says.

I have really tilted the cards in my favour, I think.
We shovel topsoil into the planter from the back of his
Tacoma pick-up. While we shovel, we talk about some of
the challenges of growing vegetables in La Ventana. I don't
have a green thumb and hang on his every word. After he
leaves, I rake the soil smooth. I mount two five-gallon water
jugs for drip irrigation. I want this garden to be as easy as
possible. My goal is to have fresh basil and tomatoes for pizza
all winter long. I plant a couple of packages of seed and go
inside.

Later, I drive to a roadside vegetable stand in Los Planes.
While bagging some oranges, Chava pulls up. He's noticed
my van from the highway.

"Hello, my friend," he says, fist-bumping me. He looks
good, which I am pleased to see.

"I wish my wife shopped here more," he says. "The
grocery stores are too expensive."

I'm pleased that he seems to still be with his wife.

"This place has the freshest fruits and vegetables," I say.

"I know I didn't do things correctly before," he says. "I
feel bad that I still owe you money."

"Can you pay me back?" I ask.

"I don't have any money," he says. "I can't find any work."

"There's a building boom in La Ventana," I say.

"The big companies don't hire me," he says, shaking his head.

That's because of your lousy reputation, I think. But I resist the urge to speak my mind.

"I could do some work for you to pay you back?" he says. "I am an honourable man."

I stop sorting oranges and look at him. He seems like the guy that started my house, not the broken-down drunk that walked away.

"I want a cement table behind my house," I say.

"How big?"

"About two meters," I say.

"That's no problem," he says. "Can we go there now?" he asks.

"Let me pay for these things." I place the plastic basin I used to hold the produce on the counter to be weighed. Chava follows me back to the house. I show him everything that had been done in his absence.

"Chingon," he says.

We scuff up the dirt where I want the table. He doesn't have money for supplies, so I gave him a hundred dollars for cement, blocks, gravel, rebar, and sand. It's a leap of faith, but I feel optimistic. An hour later, I have a pile of sand, gravel, cement, and rebar arranged neatly in my yard.

Chava shows up around ten the following morning with a young helper named Javi.

He carries a shovel and a level.

"Is this where you want the table?" he asks.

"Yeah, where we said yesterday," I say.

They dig a couple of trenches. Javi then mixes cement in a wheelbarrow with a flat tire while Chava talks on the phone. They get on both sides of the wheelbarrow and strain to carry it across the yard.

"Why don't you fix the flat tire?" I ask.

"I need to fix it, but this is okay," Chava says.

It seems ridiculous not to fix the flat. There is a tire shop nearby, and a new inner tube would cost little. But this is the way Chava works.

My back is already up with Chava. I have been through the wringer. I no longer want to have an enabling relationship. I'm pleased he wants to work off his debt. But I'm uncomfortable being around him. I tell myself he will be working outside and soon I will have an outdoor kitchen.

They pour the foundation and are done for the day. I feel skeptical that he will be back. But at ten the following morning, they arrive. Chava has a 40 oz bottle of beer in his hand, called a "Whale." Here we go again, I think. They arrange the cinderblock legs of the table. Javi mixes mortar, and they carry a full wheelbarrow to the foundation. Two stacks of cinderblocks are soon mortared in place. They drop some rebar into the cavity and fill it with mortar. They tidy up and leave a little after noon.

On the third day, they show up with some scrap plywood. They build a form to hold the concrete for the countertop. They cut the rebar and wire it into position on the top. Then they carry a couple wheelbarrow loads of wet concrete to the table. Javi shovels the mixture into the forms. Chava trowels it smooth. When they leave, Chava ask me to keep it wet, so the countertop wouldn't crack. Every couple of hours, I dump water on its surface. Chava says it will take a couple of days for the concrete to set and they will return on Saturday morning to finish up.

Since they aren't returning for a day, I decide to shop for a pizza oven. I wake early and drive to a shop in nearby San Pedro. I had driven past it many times and knew it had a selection of garden items, including barbecues and pizza ovens. When I park, the owner greets me. I tell him I'm looking for a pizza oven. He takes me to the back where there are three pizza ovens of different sizes on a counter. He says he makes pizzas regularly, and I believe him from the soot on the ovens.

"This small one is best for pizza," he says. "There's enough room for a small pizza, and you don't need too much wood."

It's a simple terracotta oven with a five-inch flue on top. It has a steel door that drops down the front. The base of the stove is steel and three steel legs support it. It's ideal, and I pay him for it. He then explains how to build a fire and then push the coals to the side. He tells me that I can bake bread or even roast things. He lifts it into the back of the van, and I celebrate with a pizza at El Triunfo Cafe.

When I get home, I position the oven next to the table. I walk to a nearby slash pile and pick up some thick branches. I light the wood, and it burns brightly. Flames swirl in the oven. I take a cornbread mix from my kitchen and add milk, eggs, a can of corn, and a chopped jalapeno. Soon, I have a fantastic treat. I'm ready to learn to make pizza.

Chava and Javi turn up Saturday morning and remove the forms. He smooths the edges of the table with a thin concrete. He stuccos the legs, and the table is finished. They then spend a couple of hours cementing rocks for a deck in front of the table. I have collected a pile of flat stones that I thought would be perfect. While I don't have many stones, I know Chava and Javi can stretch them out to make a good place to stand while cooking.

A friend invites me for a swim, and I go to the beach for a couple of hours. When I return, Javi is sleeping in the shade of the house. I go upstairs and see Chava slumbering on my couch on the deck. It's an invasion, and I resent him for it. He felt he could go into my house without asking and take a nap. I clear my throat, and Chava wakes up.

"Compa," he says.

"I guess your work is done, and you can go now," I say.

"You like it?" he asks.

"The table is good," I say.

"The problem is I don't have any money to pay my Javi," he says.

"Our deal is I only pay for materials," I respond.

"But he doesn't have any money, and he's been working all week," says Chava. "He needs to eat."

"Our deal was that you were paying off what you owe me," I say.

"But I can't honor that arrangement because I can't pay him," he says. "He has worked hard and should be paid."

I look out the window, discouraged. The men who worked for Chava sometimes complained about not being paid fully or on time.

"What does it matter?" he reasons. "You have lots of money, and he has nothing."

I know Chava is right, but it isn't my responsibility. Chava could have built the table himself without a helper. But he is lazy, and Javi did all the heavy lifting. I'm once again being manipulated.

"I will give him two hundred dollars," I say.

Chava looks relieved and without missing a beat he says, "I've got another thing to talk to you about. Your house is very beautiful, and I need to keep busy. You have many friends who want to buy land."

"I do," I agree.

"I need you to introduce them to me," he says. "I know where the best land is."

I would never refer my friends to you, I think. It dawns on me that the only reason he is at my house is to get to my friends. He brought Javi to do most of the work and he isn't interested in paying his debt.

"I know of land with good views and water," he says. "And when I get paid, I will give you the rest of the money I owe you."

He pulls a notepad out of his pocket. "If you give me their names and phone numbers, I will call them myself," he says.

"I can't do that, Chava," I say. "It's time you left."

"You can email their names later," he says, getting to his feet.

I follow Chava downstairs and give Javi the money. I thank Javi for his work, and they're gone. I walk out to the cement table. It's smooth and beautiful. The deck is a mess, however. The cement is coarse. The stones are haphazardly placed and uneven. I knew Chava's work was always highly variable. Some things would be fantastic, while others were God awful. I take a deep breath. The house has deficiencies and problems. Most jobs were done well, and some less so.

My Mexican Home

Lucas starts to surprise me with small embellishments to the house. One afternoon, he carries a pair of stools to the door. He says they will look amazing at the kitchen counter. They are made from parota, and their minimalist design is strongly Mexican. They're stout and suit my parota island countertop extension. They are exquisite.

We sit at the counter and have a beer. Many times during building, Lucas had deviated from my original idea. The result was always much better than my original intent. He would take my plans and give them a twist and always improve them. Without his help, I would still be in the weeds with Chava.

My favorite art shop is Casa Parra. Claudia, the owner, has fabulous taste and a lighthearted way. Every autumn, she suggests Christmas presents for Emily and Jessica. Her taste is always insightful, and the gifts are a hit. One lazy after-noon, I wander into her shop and see a whale mobile. It is made of aluminum rod and sea glass and is four feet long. Since it's lightweight and minimal, it will be perfect over my dining room table. The mobile fills me with joy, and I buy it on the spot.

My earliest art memory is of an Alexander Calder mobile in my bedroom as a kid. I used to spend hours watching it spin. When I was fifty, I visited the Reina Sofia Gallery in Madrid. They had a couple of impressive Calder statues in a courtyard. In the gift shop was the identical mobile I had as a kid. The whale mobile gives me a similar feeling to the Calder mobile I had watched all those years ago.

As the sun climbs into the sky, clouds fill in from the south. Soon, rain pelts the desert, swirling and drenching everything. As the kettle boils, I realize that I've left my patio door open. Walking upstairs, I see a wet woodpecker under my bed. Most days, it sits on my pergola and never seems that frightened of me. The woodpecker is drenched, and I'm not sure how to help it. I decide the best thing is to leave it alone. Since the wind is from the south, I can leave the patio door open. When the woodpecker is dry, it will leave on its own.

I go back downstairs and make a coffee. I read and watch the storm from under a fleece blanket the rest of the morning. At noon, I head upstairs. The woodpecker is oblivious to my presence. I go downstairs and get a saucer of water. I slide the water under the bed. The woodpecker's eyes are half-opened, and I'm concerned that he's injured. But knowing that there isn't more I can do, I go back downstairs.

Throughout the day, the rains come and go. I wonder if there is anything I can feed him. I go online and look for suggestions. But I'm fresh out of mealworms. Gradually, the woodpecker starts to appear fluffy. Late in the afternoon, the sun finally pierces the clouds. When I go upstairs, the woodpecker is perched on the pergola. He looks at me before launching into the air and disappearing into the forest.

As my basil and tomatoes grow, I become concerned about cows. Several are grazing nearby most days. When I don't see them, I hear their bells clanging. I park beside my house and use a three-foot gap between a couple of posts for access. I never bothered to build a gate because the cows never came into my yard. But now that the tomatoes and basil are maturing, I fear getting cleaned out. I go to the hardware store and buy a few meters of heavy chain and hasps so I can keep them out.

I get my angle grinder out of the bodega and put a zip blade on it. This thin blade allows you to cut metal quickly. I hold up the chain and estimate the amount required. I reach for the angle grinder and realize I've forgotten to bring a pair of vice grips to hold the chain while I'm cutting it. I look at the chain and think it won't be necessary because I'll be extra careful.

I start the angle grinder and bring the blade to the chain. Sparks fly, and I hold firm. A moment later, the grinder jumps. In an instant, the index finger on my left hand has a deep gash. I drop the angle grinder and stand up. Ruby-red blood starts to ooze. It doesn't hurt, and I know I'm in shock. I need a few stitches, I think. I wrap my hand in a tea towel. I get in the van and drive to the hospital in La Paz. I elevate my hand and try not to curse my foolishness. If only I had taken thirty seconds to get the vice grips.

There are three hospitals in La Paz, but the only one I have been to is the "Purple Hospital." I walk in the main entrance, and a nurse at the admitting desk leads me to an examination room. Another nurse follows and takes off the bloody tea towel. She moves a light near my hand to examine the cut. Feeling faint, I look away as a doctor enters.

"I'm Dr. Jimenez," she says, examining the cut.

"We need to have a hand specialist see this," she explains. "We need to make sure you haven't severed a tendon or a nerve or anything."

It dawns on me that the injury might be more involved than a few stitches. They leave the room, and I lay back on the bed with my hand wrapped in gauze. Ten minutes later, an older doctor enters.

"I'm a hand specialist," he says without introducing himself.

I sit up, and he moves the light close to my finger. He looks at the cut and asks me to bend my finger. Blood pumps, and he covers it with fresh gauze.

"You're fine. I don't think you cut any tendons or nerves," and he leaves the room.

I've dodged a bullet. The nurse and Dr. Jimenez return and freeze my finger with an injection in my palm. While my hand freezes, they disinfect the cut and layout the needed tools. Soon, they are threading sutures, and the gash closes. After bandaging my finger to the wrist and giving me a tetanus shot, I'm free to go.

"Thank you for taking such good care of me," I say.

The nurse leads me to the admitting desk. I sit in a chair while they prepare care instructions and antibiotics and I pay the bill of $90, which includes the removal of the stitches in ten days time.

I drive a few miles to my favorite seafood restaurant, Mariscos El Toro Guerro. I order a tall glass of Limonada and Shrimp a la Diabla, the most comforting food known to man. A mariachi band plays in the corner. I feel fortunate to be in a country that is so caring.

As I drive home, I see a banner stretched across a fence for a proposed housing development called "Calypso." It says "Joyful Living." The ad has photographs of people riding bikes, swimming, and hiking. I immediately recoil with a smug sense of resentment, like the only way to develop Baja is the way I did it. Or the way my friends are living in the campground and arroyos. I feel embarrassed. There are many ways to approach vacation living or retirement. I like my choices. But they are my choices. Others would hate my lifestyle. I don't want to be criticized, and I don't have the right to criticize others. I'm ashamed by my arrogance. I go to sleep with a throbbing hand.

I wake at five. In the darkness, I go downstairs, turn on the kettle, and make a coffee. My bandaged finger makes things more complicated. I play Jackson Browne and recline on the corner of the sofa. The dimensions of the room strike me. It feels boxy but also very homey. The proportions are perfect, I think.

I turn on my Kindle. Will I ever finish *Infinite Jest*? I wonder. Instead, I read Somerset Maugham. I'm deep into my second cup of coffee when the sun starts to rise. Wispy clouds and the first hints of orange brighten the sky. The underside of the clouds are soon a deep crimson and the horizon a glowing orange band.

I hear birds flying from tree to tree and know it's a "surge day" in the desert. I step into the chill of the yard. The woodpecker sits on top of the Rancho Relaxo sign, watching my every move. I won't see any workmen today, tomorrow, or next week. A couple walks past the yard.

"Buenos Dias," I say.

"Good morning," says the woman with an unmistakable American accent. They look athletic. The woman wears black Lululemon tights and a tank. The man wears board shorts and a t-shirt advertising a kiteboarding company.

"Is this your house?" the man asks.

"Yeah."

"It's lovely," says the woman.

"You wouldn't consider selling it?" says the man.

"I just finished her," I say. "Besides, you wouldn't want to deny yourself the adventure of building a house of your own."

A cactus wren lands on a nearby Cardon. They smile and tell me to have a good day and disappear down the path. I'm home.

Manufactured by Amazon.ca
Bolton, ON

26334727R00097